12—

MANNERISM AND ANTI-MANNERISM

IN ITALIAN PAINTING

Interpretations in Art

Interpretations in Art
A series of Columbia University Press

Paul Klee: Legends of the Sign
Rainer Crone and Joseph Koerner

WALTER FRIEDLAENDER

MANNERISM AND ANTI-MANNERISM

IN ITALIAN PAINTING

COLUMBIA UNIVERSITY PRESS

NEW YORK

Columbia University Press

New York   Oxford

Copyright © 1957, 1990 Columbia University Press

All rights reserved

Library of Congress Cataloging-in-Publication Data

Friedlaender, Walter F., 1873–1966.

Mannerism and anti-mannerism in Italian painting / Walter
Friedlaender; introduction by Donald Posner.

p.   cm.—(Interpretations in art)

ISBN 0-231-02024-4

ISBN 0-231-08388-2 (pbk.)

1. Painting, Italian. 2. Mannerism (Art)—Italy. 3. Painting,
Baroque—Italy. 4. Painting—16th century—Italy.   I. Title.

II. Series.

ND615.F7   1990

759.5'09'031—dc20

90-1840

CIP

Casebound editions of Columbia University Press books are Smyth-sewn
and printed on permanent and durable acid-free paper

∞

Printed in the United States of America

p 10 9 8 7 6 5 4 3

c 10 9 8 7 6 5 4 3 2

PRESENTED TO

WALTER FRIEDLAENDER

ON THE OCCASION OF HIS EIGHTIETH BIRTHDAY

MARCH 10, 1953

BY HIS FRIENDS AND FORMER STUDENTS, WITH THE SUPPORT OF

THE WARBURG INSTITUTE, LONDON

AND

THE ALUMNI ASSOCIATION OF THE INSTITUTE OF FINE ARTS OF

NEW YORK UNIVERSITY

CONTENTS

ILLUSTRATIONS   ix

FOREWORD   xiii
Donald Posner

ACKNOWLEDGMENTS   xxiii

THE ANTICLASSICAL STYLE   3

THE ANTI-MANNERIST STYLE   47

INDEX   85

ILLUSTRATIONS

After page 34

1 JACOPO PONTORMO: VISITATION. FLORENCE, CHIOSTRO DELL'ANNUNZIATA. *Photo by Anderson, Rome*

2 JACOPO PONTORMO: MADONNA AND CHILD WITH SAINTS. FLORENCE, S. MICHELE VISDOMINI. *Photo by Alinari, Florence*

3 JACOPO PONTORMO: VERTUMNUS AND POMONA. FLORENCE, POGGIO A CAIANO. *Photo by Alinari, Florence*

4 JACOPO PONTORMO: STUDY FOR LUNETTE DECORATION AT POGGIO A CAIANO. FLORENCE, UFFIZI. *Photo from the Office of the Photographer of the Soprintendenza alle Gallerie*

5 JACOPO PONTORMO: CHRIST BEFORE PILATE. FLORENCE, CERTOSA DEL GALLUZZO. *Photo from the Office of the Photographer of the Soprintendenza alle Gallerie*

6 JACOPO PONTORMO: PIETÀ. FLORENCE, CERTOSA DEL GALLUZZO. *Photo from the Office of the Photographer of the Soprintendenza alle Gallerie*

7 JACOPO PONTORMO: RESURRECTION. FLORENCE, CERTOSA DEL GALLUZZO. *Photo from the Office of the Photographer of the Soprintendenza alle Gallerie*

8 ROSSO FIORENTINO: ASSUMPTION OF THE VIRGIN. FLORENCE, SS. ANNUNZIATA. *Photo by Alinari, Florence*

9   ROSSO FIORENTINO: MARRIAGE OF THE VIRGIN. FLORENCE, S. LO-RENZO. *Photo by Alinari, Florence*

10 ROSSO FIORENTINO: DEPOSITION FROM THE CROSS. VOLTERRA, PINACOTECA. *Photo from the Officer of the Photographer of the Soprintendenza alle Gallerie*

11 ROSSO FIORENTINO: MOSES AND THE DAUGHTERS OF JETHRO. FLORENCE, UFFIZI. *Photo from the Office of the Photographer of the Soprintendenza alle Gallerie*

12 PARMIGIANINO: VISION OF ST. JEROME. LONDON, NATIONAL GALLERY. *Reproduced by courtesy of the Trustees, the National Gallery, London*

13 PARMIGIANINO: MADONNA DAL COLLO LUNGO. FLORENCE, PITTI. *Photo from the Office of the Photographer of the Soprintendenza alle Gallerie*

14 LODOVICO CARRACCI: MADONNA DEGLI SCALZI. BOLOGNA, PINACOTECA. *Photo by Villani and Figli, Bologna*

15 GIORGIO VASARI: IMMACULATE CONCEPTION. LUCCA, PINACOTECA. *Photo by Alinari, Florence*

16 LODOVICO CARRACCI: TRANSFIGURATION. BOLOGNA, PINACOTECA. *Photo by Anderson, Rome*

17 ROSSO FIORENTINO: TRANSFIGURATION. CITTÁ DI CASTELLO, CATHEDRAL. *Photo by Alinari, Florence*

18 ORAZIO SAMACCHINI: CORONATION OF THE VIRGIN. BOLOGNA, PINACOTECA. *Photo by Alinari, Florence*

19 ANNIBALE CARRACCI: BAPTISM OF CHRIST. BOLOGNA, S. GREGORIO. *Photo by Villani and Figli, Bologna*

20 JACOPINO DEL CONTE: BAPTISM OF CHRIST. ROME, S. GIOVANNI DECOLLATO. *Photo by Gabinetto Fotografico Nazionale, Rome*

21 SANTI DI TITO: BAPTISM OF CHRIST. FLORENCE, GALLERIA CORSINI. *Photo by Brogi, Florence*

22 SANTI DI TITO: NATIVITY. FLORENCE, S. GIUSEPPE. *Photo by Alinari, Florence*

23 ANNIBALE CARRACCI: ASSUMPTION OF THE VIRGIN. DRESDEN, GEMÄLDEGALERIE. *Photo by the Gemäldegalerie*

24 ANNIBALE CARRACCI: CHRIST IN GLORY. FLORENCE, PITTI. *Photo by Alinari, Florence*

25 ORAZIO SAMACCHINI: CHRIST IN GLORY. BOLOGNA, S. PAOLO. *Photo by Alinari, Florence*

26 CERANO: MADONNA AND CHILD WITH SAINTS. FLORENCE, UFFIZI. *Photo by Alinari, Florence*

27 RAPHAEL: CONVERSION OF ST. PAUL (TAPESTRY). ROME, VATICAN. *Photo by Alinari, Florence*

28 MICHELANGELO: CONVERSION OF ST. PAUL. ROME, VATICAN, CAPPELLA PAOLINA. *Photo by Anderson, Rome*

29 FRANCESCO SALVIATI: CONVERSION OF ST. PAUL. ROME, GALLERIA DORIA. *Photo by Alinari, Florence*

30 ERCOLE PROCACCINI: CONVERSION OF ST. PAUL. BOLOGNA, S. GIACOMO MAGGIORE. *Photo by Alinari, Florence*

31 DENIS CALVAERT: CONVERSION OF ST. PAUL (DRAWING). PARIS, LOUVRE. *Photo from the Archives photographiques, Paris*

32 DENIS CALVAERT: CONVERSION OF ST. PAUL. VIENNA, PRIVATE COLLECTION. *Photo through the courtesy of the Warburg Institute, London*

33 LODOVICO CARRACCI: CONVERSION OF ST. PAUL. BOLOGNA, PINACOTECA. *Photo by Alinari, Florence*

34 CARAVAGGIO: CONVERSION OF ST. PAUL. ROME, STA. MARIA DEL POPOLO. *Photo by Alinari, Florence*

35 CARAVAGGIO: SUPPER AT EMMAUS, MILAN, BRERA. *Photo by Brera Gallery*

36 CARAVAGGIO: SUPPER AT EMMAUS. LONDON, NATIONAL GALLERY. *Reproduced by courtesy of the Trustees, the National Gallery, London*

37 FEDERIGO BAROCCI: ST. MICHELINA. ROME, VATICAN. *Photo by Anderson, Rome*

38 FEDERIGO BAROCCI: STIGMATIZATION OF ST. FRANCIS. URBINO, GALLERY. *Photo by Gabinetto Fotografico Nazionale, Rome*

39 CIGOLI: STIGMATIZATION OF ST. FRANCIS. FLORENCE, MUSEO DI S. MARCO. *Photo by Alinari, Florence*

40 CIGOLI: ST. FRANCIS IN PRAYER. FLORENCE, PITTI. *Photo by Anderson, Rome*

41 LODOVICO CARRACCI: MADONNA OF THE ROSARY. BOLOGNA, PINACOTECA. *Photo by Villani and Figli, Bologna*

42 LODOVICO CARRACCI: MARTYRDOM OF ST. ANGELO. BOLOGNA, PINACOTECA. *Photo by Alinari, Florence*

43 LODOVICO CARRACCI: MADONNA APPEARING TO ST. HYACINTH. PARIS, LOUVRE. *Photo from the Archives photographiques, Paris*

44 LODOVICO CARRACCI: ST. CHARLES BORROMEO BEFORE THE SARCOPHAGUS IN VARALLO. BOLOGNA, S. BARTOLOMMEO. *Photo by Villani and Figli, Bologna*

45 CERANO: MADONNA WITH ST. CHARLES BORROMEO AND ST. AMBROGIO. PAVIA, CERTOSA. *Photo through the courtesy of the Warburg Institute, London*

46 CRESPI: THE MEAL OF ST. CHARLES BORROMEO. MILAN, CHIESA DELLA PASSIONE. *Photo by Alinari, Florence*

FOREWORD

WALTER FRIEDLAENDER was one of the pioneers in the modern exploration of sixteenth century Italian art. The two essays in this book by Professor Friedlaender were among the first to chart the boundaries and to define the character of the periods that are now generally called Mannerist and early Baroque; almost forty years old at this printing, these essays are still essential guides for students of these fields.

The first study, of the "anticlassical style," was originally published in 1925, but it had already been presented by Professor Friedlaender in 1914 as his inaugural address at the University of Freiburg. At that time, knowledge and appreciation of sixteenth century Italian art were, for the most part, limited to the High Renaissance. The general view of the art and artists that came after such giants as Raphael and Michelangelo had, in essentials, remained unchanged since its original formulation in the seventeenth century. (Cf., for instance, Gian Pietro Bellori, *Le Vite dei pittori* . . . , Rome, 1672, p. 20.) The years from the end of the High Renaissance until about 1600 were considered a period of artistic decline brought about by a servile, uncritical imitation of the manners of the great masters, and especially of the anatomical exaggerations of Michelangelo's figure style. Seventeenth century writers had used the word *maniera* ("manner" or "mode") to

describe the art of the later sixteenth century because of its dependence on artificial and derivative representational formulae
that depart from natural appearances. Thus, "Mannerism" even-
tually became the usual term for the style that followed the High
Renaissance.

At the beginning of this century Mannerist art was still thought
to have no historical importance. Indeed, Heinrich Wölfflin, whose
Principles of Art History (English translation, New York, 1932)
appeared in 1915—a year after Professor Friedlaender gave his
lecture on the anticlassical style—disregarded Mannerism and
postulated an uninterrupted evolution from the classical style of
the Renaissance to the baroque style of the seventeenth century.
Professor Friedlaender was one of a small number of scholars
around 1915 who began to investigate Mannerism seriously. These
men were largely inspired by the writings of Alois Riegl, who had
shown that the art of supposedly decadent periods could be inter-
preted in terms of positive, although non-classical, expressive
purposes. Riegl demonstrated his thesis in magistral studies of
late Roman art (1901) and of Baroque art (1908), but it was left
for a younger generation to reinterpret the art of Mannerism.
It has frequently been remarked that the "discovery" of Mannerism
coincided with the development of expressionistic and abstract
modes in modern art. Certainly, the experience of the contemporary
artistic revolt against naturalistic representation contributed greatly
to an appreciation and comprehension of the apparently similar
intentions of Mannerist artists. In 1919 Werner Weisbach, while
taking a negative approach to Mannerism, stressed its abstracting,
stylizing mentality ("Der Manierismus," *Zeitschrift für bildende
Kunst,* XXX), and in a brilliant lecture in 1920 Max Dvořák
analyzed the subjective, expressionistic intentions of Mannerism,
which he saw as manifestations of a general "spiritual crisis" in the
sixteenth century ("El Greco and Mannerism"; English translation in *Magazine of Art,* XLVI, no. 1, 1953. A full discussion of
Mannerism was given by Dvořák in courses at the University of

Vienna in 1918-1920, and published posthumously in his *Geschichte der italienischen Kunst im Zeitalter der Renaissance,* Munich, 1927-1929, II.).

Although he made many of the same observations as Weisbach and Dvořák, Professor Friedlaender approached the problem of Mannerism in a more rigorous and perhaps more far-reaching historical manner. He made a masterful analysis of the main characteristics of early Mannerist art—irrational spatial constructions, figural elongation, etc.—and argued that they represent a deliberate denial of the classical aesthetic rather than the result of continued imitation of Renaissance forms. For this reason he suggested the term "anticlassical style," which stressed the character of artistic revolt that he considered crucial to the opening phase of the Mannerist period. Around 1910 the chronological limits of Mannerism were still only vaguely defined. One placed the beginning of the period about 1530 or 1540 and its end about 1600. However, by a close examination of the art of the first decades of the sixteenth century, Professor Friedlaender was able to recognize earlier manifestations of the "anticlassical" spirit and to fix the origins of the Mannerist style precisely around 1520. For the first time artists like Rosso, Pontormo, and Parmigianino were put forward prominently as creators of Mannerism, and this led to an important reappraisal of the significance and quality of their art. In a similar way, Michelangelo's late paintings in the Sistine and Pauline Chapels in the Vatican Palace could now be seen in a new and more meaningful context. They no longer appeared as the eccentric products of the master's old age and as the corrupting influence on the younger generation, but as major statements of the anticlassical aesthetic of the time.

The new precision given to the definition of Mannerism has necessarily affected our idea of the High Renaissance period that preceded it. Long thought to have been in comfortable domination of almost half the sixteenth century, High Renaissance style is now seen as maintaining a somewhat tenuous grasp on a period of only about twenty years. Furthermore, as Professor Friedlaender pointed out, "every artistic epoch prepares the next," and in the classic period there are "storm signals" that indicate the approach of Mannerism. A number of scholars have since looked at Renaissance style with this in mind; most recently, the idea of a gathering crisis in High Renaissance art is found as one of the leitmotifs of S. J. Freedberg's monumental study, *Painting of the High Renaissance in Rome and Florence* (Cambridge, 1961).

When he chose the term "anticlassical," Professor Friedlaender considered a special connotation that it had at the time. The term was being used to describe qualities of German painting; Professor Friedlaender, who began his essay by pointing to Pontormo's debt to Dürer, thus emphasized the connection of Mannerism with other artistic phenomena that were not wholly or at all in sympathy with High Renaissance classicism. The relation of the Italian anticlassical style to "Gothic" art, and the persistence of "Gothic" elements in the Renaissance period, noted by Professor Friedlaender, have been subjects of great interest to scholars in the field. (See, for instance, F. Antal in *Jahrbuch der Preussischen Kunstsammlungen,* XLVI, 1925; *Kritische Berichte zur Kunstgeschichtlichen Literatur,* I/II, 1928/29; and G. S. Adelmann and G. Weise, *Das Fortleben gotischer Ausdrucks- und Bewegungsmotive in der Kunst des Manierismus,* Tübingen, 1954.)

Although Professor Friedlaender considered the creation of Mannerism an essentially Tuscan accomplishment, he pointed out that there are recognizable features of Mannerism in the Raphael school. He also called attention to the spread of manneristic trends in Italy and, beyond the borders of Italy, to France and other northern countries. However, he does not seem to have anticipated the extraordinary "metastasis" of our concept of Mannerism that has occurred since the 1920's. Artists like Peter Bruegel have come to be explained as Mannerist (see, for instance, O. Benesch, *The Art of the Renaissance in Northern Europe,* Cambridge, 1947, a work much indebted to Max Dvořák) in the course of an effort to tie all European art and culture between about 1520 and about 1590 into an "age of Mannerism." This expansionistic trend culminated in 1955 in the great exhibition called "The Triumph of European Mannerism," organized in Amsterdam and sponsored by the Council of Europe. A number of recent popular and semi-popular books have advertised this rather catholic concept of Mannerism, although many scholars today are wary of the over-simplifications that such a view involves and tend to follow Professor Friedlaender's lead by focusing on the distinctive character of artistic and cultural movements in specific places and at specific times.

One of Professor Friedlaender's major points was the distinction he made between a first and second phase within the period of Mannerism itself. (This distinction is most clearly stated in the second essay in this book, on the "anti-mannerist" style.) The art of later Mannerism, which has come to be called by the original term, "Maniera," (the word for Mannerism in contemporary Italian is "il Manierismo") was considered by Professor Friedlaender imitative, a kind of "mannered" Mannerism that merely exaggerated, and thereby vitiated, the creative anticlassicism of early Mannerism. The division of Mannerism into two separate periods is now almost universally accepted, although today one tends to place the beginning of the second period around 1530 rather than around 1550 as Professor Friedlaender suggested. However, in the last few years there have been major efforts to reassess the meaning and quality of both moments of Mannerism. In a remarkable study by Craig Hugh Smyth the later, "maniera" style has been shown to proceed from aesthetic ideals that are quite distinct from, and to some extent even incompatible with, the earlier, Tuscan anticlassical style. (*Mannerism and* MANIERA, Locust Valley, New York, 1963; here, incidentaly, the reader will find a full critical discussion of the literature on Mannerism.) John Shearman takes a similar position in an important paper, *"Maniera as an Aesthetic Ideal,"* (*Studies in Western Art* [Acts of the

Twentieth Congress of the History of Art], 1963, II). Both authors would also define the character of the new style around 1520 and its relation to the art of the High Renaissance in a different way from Professor Friedlaender, stressing stylistic continuities rather than aesthetic revolt; and neither is happy about using the term Mannerism for the early "anticlassical style" in Tuscany. Thus, our concepts of Mannerism are still fluid and we are still engaged in the art historical colloquy that Professor Friedlaender did so much to initiate and to which his penetrating insights still contribute.

The second essay in this book, originally published in 1930 (although written several years earlier), complements the first by investigating how the Mannerist period was brought to an end. In the first quarter of this century a good deal of work was done on the origins and precedents of seventeenth century Italian style. (For the state of art historical knowledge in the 1920's of the Mannerist and post-Mannerist periods, see the classic survey by Nikolaus Pevsner, *Die italienische Malerei vom Ende der Renaissance bis zum ausgehenden Rokoko* [Handbuch der Kunstwissenschaft, Wildpark-Potsdam, 1928.]). It had long been recognized that a change of direction occurred in Italian painting around 1590. Professor Friedlaender, however, attempted to determine the scope and the precise character of this change. His analysis showed that a new style appeared suddenly, and that it was, from the first, sharply opposed to the basic premises of Mannerism. These facts suggested a correspondance between the "style of 1590" and the anticlassical style of 1520, since both movements could be seen as products of a reaction to dominant ideals of the period that immediately preceded them. Hence, Professor Friedlaender proposed the term "anti-mannerist" to describe the new style of the last decades of the sixteenth century. Just as the anticlassical style tended to return to the "Gothic" currents in pre-High Renaissance art, so the anti-mannerist style, in reaction to Mannerism, showed a profound sympathy for the art of the High Renaissance. In Professor Friedlaender's view the negativistic and retrospective character of both anticlassicism and anti-mannerism can be explained by the tendency of a generation to revolt against the principles and teachings of its fathers and to take up the ideals of its "grandfathers." Recently, the idea of deliberate stylistic opposition to Mannerism in developments around 1590 has been less emphasized by some writers than the relation of the art of the time to already existing subordinate or peripheral trends. (Cf. F. Zeri, *Pittura e Controriforma,* Turin, 1957.) Indeed, Professor Friedlaender himself hinted at the possibility of this approach by calling attention to the conservative, academic undercurrent in late Mannerism represented by an artist like Santi di Tito, who seems to anticipate the anti-mannerist style by twenty or twenty-five years.

Of primary importance is the emphasis Professor Friedlaender placed on the fact that various artists in different centers of Italy began simultaneously to explore new stylistic directions around 1580 or 1590. For the most part these artists did not influence each other, and their personal styles are to a great extent visually dissimilar. For these reasons many scholars have not remarked the internal coherence of the period around 1590, and have classified Barocci and Cerano as Mannerists in contrast to the Carracci and Caravaggio, who are usually considered early, or pre-Baroque. However, Professor Friedlaender recognized in the new works of the time a common attitude *vis-a-vis* Mannerism, and in his essay he made a brilliant demonstration of this community by focusing on a critical point of reference for the anti-mannerist style. He reasoned that since Mannerism could be understood as a subjective, "spiritual" style, it should be precisely in the representation of "transcendental" themes that the artists of the late sixteenth century would most clearly manifest their anti-mannerist attitudes and reveal the essential coherence of the new artistic spirit. (The original title of Professor Friedlaender's essay was, significantly, "The Anti-Mannerist Style around 1590 and its Relation to the Transcendental.") The result of his analysis and comparison of various treatments of religious subjects is that a whole group of artists from Barocci to Caravaggio suddenly appear to stand apart from Mannerism. Professor Friedlaender expressed the essential difference between their art and the art of the Mannerists with utmost sensitivity and precision: in representations of sacred subjects "Mannerism sought for the most far-reaching removal from everything earthly, for something purely speculative"; in the new style "both miracles and visions were . . . placed in man's closest and demonstrable surroundings, or even in his own heart." Despite the great individual differences in their means of pictorial expression, and despite the persistence of mannerist devices in some of their art, this group of painters working around 1590 appear united in a general trend toward greater pictorial immediacy and directness in dramatic presentation.

The relation of Mannerist and Baroque art to contemporary religious movements was a much debated question in the 1920's. (See especially, W. Weisbach, *Der Barock als Kunst der Gegenreformation,* Berlin, 1921; N. Pevsner, "Gegenreformation und Manierismus," *Repertorium für Kunstwissenschaft,* XLVI, 1925; W. Weisbach, "Gegenreformation-Manierismus-Barock," *ibid.,* XLIX, 1928.) In his essay Professor Friedlaender was able to call attention to some of the specific connections that link the anti-mannerist style to the new religious spirit that orders like the Franciscans and that such reformers as St. Charles Borromeo were fostering at the time. More recently, Professor Friedlaender has further clarified this relationship in his *Caravaggio Studies* (Princeton, 1955, Chapter VI). Although Professor Friedlaender stressed the unity and originality of the anti-mannerist period, he also pointed out its fundamental importance for the art of the next century. However, he showed that the art and the "spirit" of the years around 1590 were distinct from what came later, and he argued cogently that the anti-mannerist period must be considered *sui generis,* and not equated with a seventeenth century "age of the Baroque."

A final word must be said about the scholarly method that informs both of the essays in this book. Professor Friedlaender avoids the chilling aestheticism of abstract style analysis as well as the vagueness of methods that seek analogies between generalized tendencies in art and other cultural phenomena. The originality of his approach, perhaps best illustrated here in the essay on the anti-mannerist style, is based on his ability to grasp the precise repercussions of different stylistic events for the dramatic and narrative content of a work of art. In the second essay, he selected subjects, such as the *Conversion of St. Paul,* that had deep spiritual significance for the sixteenth century. By analyzing the way that these themes were represented at different moments during the century he was able to trace the migration of artistic consciousness from the High Renaissance to the pre-Baroque period. Today, as forty years ago, these essays offer not only important historical insights, but a lucid and graceful demonstration of an exemplary art historical method.

DONALD POSNER

Institute of Fine Arts
New York University
December 7, 1964

ACKNOWLEDGMENTS

THESE two essays appeared in *Repertorium für Kunstwissenschaft,* Vol. XLVII, 1925, and in *Vorträge der Bibliothek,* Warburg, XIII, 1929. They are presented here in translations, with few revisions in content, prepared by the collaboration of my friends and students: Jane Costello, Creighton Gilbert, Robert Goldwater, Frederick Hartt, Dora Jane Janson, and Mahonri S. Young. I should also like to thank those who collaborated in the editing: William Crelly, Magda Keesal, and Robert O. Parks.

THE ANTICLASSICAL STYLE

IN HIS LIFE of Jacopo da Pontormo, Vasari speaks approximately as follows of the frescoes in the Certosa: "For Pontormo to have imitated Dürer in his motifs (*invenzioni*) is not in itself reprehensible. Many painters have done so and still do. In this he certainly did not go astray. However, it is extremely regrettable that he took over the German manner lock, stock, and barrel, down to the facial expression and even in movement. For through this infiltration of the German manner his original early manner, which was full of beauty and grace and which with his innate feeling for beauty he had completely mastered, was transformed from the ground up and utterly wiped out. In all his works under the influence of the German manner, only slight traces are recognizable of the high quality and the grace which had previously belonged to his figures."

As an artist Vasari is a mannerist of a strict Michelangelesque vein. But as a writer he is for the most part nonpartisan and in general much more benevolent than critical. His harsh words against Pontormo's imitation of Dürer are surely an expression not only of his own opinion, but also of the general opinion of the public. There was a feeling abroad, quite aside from any nationalism, that a major step had been taken here, one fraught with consequences. Vasari saw perfectly correctly that the imitation of Dürer on Pontormo's part involved not merely single features and the imitation of separate motifs, as was the case for Pontormo's teacher, Andrea del Sarto, but rather something fundamental, a change of style which threatened the whole structure of Renaissance painting. And yet Vasari did not see deeply enough. It was not Dürer's woodcuts and engravings—which just at that point had come to Florence in a large shipment and (as Vasari elsewhere records) which were very much admired by all artists—that were leading to such a radical change in Pontormo's artistic attitude; rather it was the reverse. The new way of feeling germinating in him, but not in him alone, permitted the young and popular artist to cling to Dürer's graphic work because it appeared as something akin to his own feeling and usable in his reaction against the ideal of the High Renaissance.

In spite of the short span of barely twenty years in which it ran its course, the particularly intensive epoch of the High Renaissance had no unified character. The very fact that Michelangelo's art cannot possibly be counted in with the "classic" art of Leonardo, Raphael, Fra Bartolommeo, and Andrea del Sarto destroys any unity. Taken strictly, there actually remains only a relatively small number of works in which the normativeness and balance of high classic style can be demonstrated. It is not my purpose here to distinguish between this classic style and the preceding trends of the *quattrocento*. It might just be remarked that in the painting of the *quattrocento* the dissociation between constructed space in depth and picture surface with figures is for the most part not yet overcome. The volume of the bodies, inwardly organized and enlivened by a central idea, is in most cases not yet set in a circular movement as it is in the drawings of Leonardo or in the Madonnas of the mature Raphael (in contrast to Perugino). In the *quattrocento* the linkage of this volume with the space is for the most part incomplete and in many phases, especially during the second half of the century, often contradictory: for the human figure, there is spiritualization and surface ornamentation; for the space, realism and perspective construction in depth. The resolution of this duality, the subordination of masses and space within one central idea, is the achievement of the High Renaissance, reflected most purely in the works of the mature period of Raphael.

At the same time, both in theory and practice, definite rules and norms (first solidly codified, however, only in much later academic classicistic circles) were created, in large part in adherence to antiquity, and especially to its sculpture. To these the proportions, the internal and outward movement, and such, of the object in nature were subordinated. Thus there arose an "ideal art" which, however, at the same time laid claims on nature, indeed in a strikingly canonical sense. Only what this artistic attitude set up as right and proper in proportions and the like counted as beautiful and, even more than that, as the only thing truly natural. On the basis of this idealized and normative objectivization, the individual object of the classic style, especially the figure of man, was removed formally, in its organization, and psychically, in its gestures and expression, from any subjective, purely optical, impression. It was no longer exposed to the more subjective whim of the individual artist, but was heightened and idealized to something objective and regular.

Sharply opposed in many and basic elements to this high, idealistic, normative attitude which in Florence (aside from Raphael) Fra Bartolommeo presents in a somewhat stiffly dogmatic way, and Andrea del Sarto in a more conciliatory, easy-going and happily colorful fashion, stands the attitude of the anticlassical style,[1] normally called Mannerism.

[1] In using the expression "anticlassical" as a label of the new style around 1520, I have not overlooked the purely negative character of this term. However, the contrast of this term to the "classicism" of the High Renaissance seemed to me justified in order to describe the beginning of the new period. It is well known that the usual term "Mannerism" originally had a derogative meaning, so that it by no means embraced the essence of the new movement. Yet a decided

What is decisive is the changed relationship of this new artistic outlook to the artistically observed object. No longer, as in idealistic standardized art, does the possibility of observing an object in a generalized intersubjective way, by heightening it, and raising it to something canonical and regular, form art's immovable basis. Similarly, little attention is paid to individually conditioned variations produced by the outward circumstances of light, air, and distance. The mannerist artist, in the last analysis, has the right or duty to employ any possible method of observation only as the basis for a new free representational variant. It, in turn, is distinguished in principle from all other possibilities of seeing an object, for it is neither made valid by any standardized abstraction nor is it casually determined in an optical way, but answers only to its own conditions. This art too is idealistic, but it does not rest on an idea of a canon, rather upon a "fantastica idea non appogiata all'imitazione," an imaginative idea unsupported by imitation of nature. Thus the canon apparently given by nature and hence generally recognized as law is definitively given up. It is no longer a question of creating a seen object in an artistically new way, "just as one sees it," or, if idealistically heightened and ethically stressed, "just as one ought to see it." Neither is it a matter of recreating the object "as I see it," as the individual person observes it as a form of appearance. Rather, if one may use a negative expression, it is to be recreated "as one does not see it," but as, from purely autonomous artistic motives, one would have it seen.

Out of the object given through artistic observation there thus arises a new and strikingly different one. The form of appearance, heretofore canonical, commonly recognized in an intersubjective

---

tendency away from this pejorative attitude has occurred even with the word "manneristic," just as happened in the cases of the terms "Gothic" or "Baroque" —a tendency which seems to indicate a greater and more general understanding of the positive values of the style.

The present essay grew out of an inaugural lecture at the University of Freiburg in the spring of 1914.

way and hence counted upon as something one could take for granted—as "natural," is given up in favor of a new, subjective, "unnatural" creation. Thus in mannerist art the proportions of the limbs can be stretched, more or less capriciously, merely out of a particular rhythmic feeling of beauty. The length of the head changes from being between an eighth and a ninth of the whole, as had been usual in the Renaissance because this was the norm and the average given by nature, and is now often between a tenth and a twelfth of the body length. This was a thoroughgoing change then, and almost a distortion of the form or appearance of an object commonly recognized as valid. Even such particular affectations as the holding of a finger, the wrenching of the limbs which twine in and out among each other, can be traced to this quite conscious rejection of the normative and the natural through an almost exclusive employment of rhythmic feeling. This freer and apparently more capricious rhythm carries with it the fact that symmetry, that is to say the linkage of parts of the body as they cohere through direct, clearly grasped opposition and distribution of weights, is dislodged or more or less broken up.[2] (Compare further below Pontormo's *Madonna and Child with Saints* in San Michele Visdomini.) The High Renaissance's regular, symmetrical harmony of parts becomes unbearable to the anticlassical style. Linkage occurs through a more or less subjective rhythmic distribution of weights, which, under some circumstances, does not exclude a quite strict ornamental ordering; in extreme cases even thrust and dissonance are hazarded. All this (as strikes us especially in the early Pontormo) gives the impression that this new form of art is consciously returning to an apparently more primitive stage, since

[2] One might be tempted to use the word "eurythmy" for this since, in ancient art terminology, εὐρυθμία stands in a certain opposition to συμμετρία, but eurythmy too, in ancient times, serves in the last analysis only for the purposes of the canonical; thus, changes in proportion in statues which were placed high up had basically only the purpose of producing a standardized impression. Cf. also the passage on the armor in Xenophon, *Memorabilia* (III, 10, 9).

it partly relinquishes the proud achievements of the Renaissance.[3] In adherence to something earlier, there is being formed a new artistic feeling, which forcibly turns aside from the previous normative one of the Renaissance. Thus there arises a new beauty, no longer resting on real forms measurable by the model or on forms idealized on this basis, but rather on an inner artistic reworking on the basis of harmonic or rhythmical requirements.

The relation of this new artistic viewpoint to the problem of space is especially interesting and important. An upholder of the normative, who feels in a classic way, will take for granted an unambiguous, constructed space in which equally unambiguous fixed figures move and act. It is not familiar, visual space dissolved in light and air, for the most part optically judged, that the adherent of the normative strives for, but a space which expresses or should express a higher reality purified of everything accidental. However, the figures of the rhythmic anticlassical painter function otherwise, for in themselves they express neither an established rule of nature, nor any unambiguous rationally understood space. In a word, for them the problem of three-dimensional space vanishes, or can do so. The volumes of the bodies more or less displace the space, that is, they themselves create the space. This already implies that an art of purely flat surfaces is as little involved here as one which is perspective and spatial. A certain effect of depth is often achieved through adding up layers of volumes of this sort, along with an evasion of perspective. In the struggle between picture surface and presentation of depth in space, which is of such vital importance throughout the whole history of art, this is a particularly interesting solution. A peculiarly unstable situation is created: the stress on the surfaces, on the picture planes, set behind each other in relief layers, does not permit any very plastic or three-dimensional volumes of the bodies to come through in full force,

---

[3] How far tendencies of the *quattrocento* are actually picked up, and how these acquire essentially other meanings in anticlassical manneristic art is still to be investigated.

while at the same time it hinders the three-dimensional bodies from giving any very flat impression.[4] (Something similar is encountered, with a somewhat different aim, in classicistic art.)

Yet even in the cases where a strong effect of depth is desired or is inevitable, the space is not constructed in the Renaissance sense as a necessity for the bodies but often is only an incongruous accompaniment for the bunches of figures, which one must read together "by jumps" in order to reach the depth. In such cases the space is not adapted to the figures as in high classic art, but is an unreal space, just as the figures are "anormal," that is, unreal. This is accompanied by another important difference from *quattrocento* art. In the fifteenth century the landscape responds to real facts and to effects of depth (partly obtained through perspective means); the bodies, on the other hand, often remain unreal and relatively flat. In the High Renaissance we see this contradiction resolved in favor of a common harmony of figures and space. In anticlassic Mannerism the figures remain plastic and have volume even if they are unreal in the normative sense, while space, if it is present at all apart from the volumes, is not pushed to the point where it produces an effect of reality. This is also true, for example, of the figure paintings of El Greco where, in spite of their coloristic tendency, the space always has something irrational and illogically organized about it. (One might cite the space and the proportions to each other of the foreground and middle-distance figures in such a work as the *St. Maurice*.)

In the Florentine aspect of Mannerism, the cult of bodily volume is often so much emphasized, and the suppression of the spatial, of the "ambiente," is so strong, that both architecture and landscape only play small roles as coulisses. The art of *disegno* tending toward

[4] In contemporary architectural ornament too (for example in church façades) the surface acquires a stronger relief in a three-dimensional sense. Depth, however, is only obtained through the things themselves, through the interlocking and the shuttling back and forth of the architectural and the ornamental members, not, as in the *seicento,* through movement and space. The same thing applies to grotesque ornament.

the abstract, that art of inward and outward design so much cele-brated toward the end of the period in various theoretical writings such as the *Idea* of Federigo Zuccaro (but also playing a part in Vasari), triumphs over the spatial ideal of the Renaissance.

The whole bent of anticlassic art is basically subjective, since it would construct and individually reconstruct from the inside out, from the subject outward, freely, according to the rhythmic feeling present in the artist, while classic art, socially oriented, seeks to crystallize the object for eternity by working out from the regular, from what is valid for everyone.[5]

In this pure subjectivism, the mannerist anticlassical current is similar to the attitudes of the late Gothic; the verticalism, the long proportions, are common to both tendencies, in contrast to the standardized balance of forms in the Renaissance. How decidedly the new movement, with its thoroughly anticlassical tone, tries in both spirit and form to approach the Gothic feeling (never com-pletely overcome even by the Renaissance), we see in the works of Jacopo da Pontormo, the true reformer of that artistic period, and in the uncompromising shock which his reversal produced in the public and in the critics, as shown in the passage from Vasari previ-ously cited.

It goes without saying that every artistic epoch prepares the next, and that here once again are to be found powerful elements of its predecessor. The so-called early Renaissance, in spite of its greater freedom with regard to the object in nature, contains in many of

[5] "Optical" art in a narrower sense is only subjective in a conditional way, for it starts out from the subject from the single individual, but wishes to establish the object even if seen *à travers*. The word "subjective" is used by Alois Riegl in this more materialistic sense. The object is presented in the way that the artist believes it actually strikes his retina as an artistic form. It also plays upon the subjective status of the observer since it requires from him activity, transfor-mation, and reaction, as for example, in foreshortenings. Yet the word "sub-jective" can also be applied in a purely spiritual sense, in the sense of a will to free construction, unobjectively, as it is in Mannerism.

its phases much that is still medieval.[6] Likewise, despite their antagonism, the anticlassic or manneristic style, and the High Renaissance have many and fundamental things in common: the preference, for example, for a plastic, anatomical treatment of the body, which in certain circles is particularly cultivated and exaggerated; their desire for a strongly tied composition; and so on. In such ways Mannerism is linked with the preceding Renaissance, especially if one sets it beside the loosening of organization that occurs in the outspoken Baroque. Yet these relationships, which are only natural, do not go so far as to justify labeling this manneristic style a late Renaissance, or treating it as a decay of the Renaissance, as has been done until quite recently even though this is entirely contrary to every older tradition. The contemporaries and even more the direct successors of Mannerism, as well as the classicists of the seventeenth century, sensed the sharp and painful division from the High Renaissance. This art-historical merger of the two styles was only possible because too little attention was paid to the whole period, or because of ignorance of its new tone, as shown in the radical reversal of its attitude to space and proportions. With greater accuracy one might have called the strong tendency of early Baroque a late Renaissance or neo-Renaissance, for in it (again in strong contrast with the preceding period of Mannerism), is to be found a conscious and intentional readoption of the Renaissance idea (again without being able to slough off completely the achievements of Mannerism).

Every revolution turns into an evolution if one assembles the preceding storm signals in a pragmatic way. Hence it ought not to be difficult to point out certain signposts of Mannerism in the mainstream of *quattrocento* art. Nor should it be forgotten that the victory of the High Renaissance was by no means complete and final, that a "latent Gothic" or a "latent Mannerism," (depending

[6] On this point, cf. the book by August Schmarsow, *Gotik in der Renaissance* (Stuttgart, 1921), which is rich in observations.

on whether one looks forward or back) was present even in the mature period of "classic" thought. Yet it is essential to establish that such an anticlassical revolution did in fact take place, datable almost exactly shortly after the death of Raphael; that a thoroughly new spiritual turn of the methods of expression emerged (which as far as I know has until now received no attention or no intensive stress); and finally that this movement was extensive, flaming up at various separate points and for a considerable period dominating the once triumphant spirit of the classic. First, however, we must clarify the relationship of the greatest genius of the time—who was anticlassical right in the middle of the classic period—to this new trend, and his connection with it.

Just as Michelangelo has been labeled the "father of the Baroque," he has also been set at the head of the mannerist movement and blamed for all the alleged sins which classicism assigned to the anticlassical style. There is justification for this, but only in a limited way. Obviously Michelangelo is not the sole creator of the new style, in the sense that all artists of this trend at his time and after are exclusively dependent on him and on his intimidating and powerful greatness. An individual, be he even as great and "terrible" as Michelangelo, can not produce a whole artistic trend by himself and from himself. Even the greatest personality is bound by many threads to his time and to its stylistic development, creating it and created by it in a complex interaction. It is thus with Rembrandt and his chiaroscuro, and thus with Goethe whose *Wilhelm Meister* carried on the romantic movement by which it was itself in turn stamped. The *Last Judgment,* that overwhelming paradigm of Mannerism which is usually set at the forefront of the movement and to which is ascribed the blame for the alleged errors of the whole trend, was painted at the end of the thirties when works as important and characteristic of the new style as those of Pontormo, Rosso, and Parmigianino had been long since produced and when hardly an artist could still escape the frenzy of the new expressive style.

Even the elongation of the figures and distortions of proportion so characteristic of Mannerism turn up quite late in Michelangelo's work. His earlier Florentine figures of Bacchus, David, and the Doni *Madonna,*[7] are altogether normally formed, indeed rather stocky than elongated in Gothic fashion. The same applies to the figures for the Julius tomb and in the Sistine, in spite of the forms of giant limbs; as an example, note the *Ignudi*. A change really first sets in when Michelangelo is again living in the service of the Medici in Florence, the breeding place of Mannerism. Yet it is not a case of a radical reversal, for this change actually involves in an active way only two figures, the Medici *Madonna* and the so-called *Victor*. They are the typical forms of expression of the mannerist side of Michelangelo's art, and as such certainly functioned as intensively "modern" and had a corresponding influence. The *Victor* especially is really the mannerist figure par excellence, with his screw-like upward thrust, his long, stretched-out, athlete's leg, his small Lysippian head, and his regular, large-scale, somewhat empty features. On the other hand both the *Victor* and the Medici *Madonna* are only by-products alongside the great works of the period, the *Times of Day* of the Medici Chapel, which like the Dukes too, are not exaggeratedly elongated in their proportions, even if they are endowed with certain marks of the new movement. It is notable furthermore that Michelangelo does not cling to the long proportions of the *Victor* and the Medici *Madonna* but that about the same period—before or around 1530—the figure of the "David—Apollo" is produced, with quite different and even strik-

[7] The early works of Michelangelo, especially the cartoon of the *Bathing Soldiers,* are, to be sure, of great significance for all artists of the period, but more in the formal aspect of their construction and movement of bodies. The Doni *Madonna* too, has little to do with the beginnings of the style, in spite of the strong affinity it has with certain tendencies of later Florentine Mannerism in the artificiality of its movement and in the peculiarly cold presentation of color with changing tones.

cky proportions. It is like the Christ of the *Last Judgment*, o be sure is still broader and more massive. In the other too of this work, so typically mannerist in many aspects, lengthened proportions do not generally dominate. Only in the groups of the patriarchs, the Adam and the others to the right and left of Christ, do long, stretched-out bodies come into view. Nor in the last frescoes of Michelangelo, in the Cappella Paolina, are they especially frequent. Only in the impressive fragment of the Rondanini *Pietà,* with the limbs that have become so thin, does the feeling of verticalism break out again in a quite remarkably Gothic way. Thus the shiftings of proportions in this manneristic direction show up in Michelangelo for the first time around 1525 to 1530, and have no important development in the style of his old age. One might almost be tempted to consider figures like the *Victor* as an unconscious concession to Mannerism, especially as regards proportion.

But that there is a more penetrating connection between Michelangelo and the anticlassical trend is proved by the fact that in architecture he shows outspoken anticlassical peculiarities just during the critical period of the end of the twenties and the beginning of the thirties. Without being able here to go into the matter more analytically, I will only point to the fact that in the architectural parts of the Julius tomb and in the Sistine such tendencies were not present, or at least not so strongly (certain interpenetrations in the Sistine do, to be sure, move in that direction), while on the other hand, one can, quite apart from the architecture of the Medici Chapel, consider the anteroom of the Laurentian Library with its staircase, in its intertwinings and narrowing of space and proportion, as the peak of manneristic architecture, and associate it directly with the *Victor* of the same period. One strong impulse within Michelangelo's artistic will as it developed in this period was thus closely tied up with the modern trend of the times, directed toward overcoming Renaissance qualities.

The same applies to composition and organization of space, except that here the genius of Michelangelo shows the way in which the anticlassical movement is going to proceed much earlier and much more effectively. The mature Michelangelo as a sculptor aims above all to prevent his figures from being surrounded by an airy space and capable of free movement. He wishes rather to make them "prisoners of the block" and, going even further, to tie them up in architectonic prison cells (as in the case of the famous locked-in columns of the Laurentian Library). The strongest psychological impulses meet insuperable pressure and resistance—they are denied space in which to expand. Thus there arises no solution to the conflict, which, precisely for this reason, operates all the more tensely and expressively. The strife of psychic and motor forces can only be resolved outside the block or its casing in a suppositional space, where the energies of the imprisoned organism continue and are dissipated. This tragic fate, so completely un-antique was only realizable through the experience of Christianity. Michelangelo also carries this over into the field of painting. The gigantic figures of the prophets and sibyls of the Sistine ceiling live and act in such a space, fearfully narrowed, almost canceled, and their powerful expansiveness points toward liberation only in a transcendental and divine space. Also in compositions of many figures where the expression of individual inwardness was less important than representation of outward emotions, Michelangelo could bring into play this artistic method—the mutual compression of energies through more or less complete renunciation of space. This happens above all in the spandrels of the Sistine ceiling, which are usually less observed than the central scenes. The small surface to be organized and the remarkable form of the triangular spandrel, difficult to cope with, called for a certain restriction in any case. But it could have been removed by illusionistic effects of depth and space, or have been brought into a kind of balance by a classically spatial plastic composition. To Michelangelo, however, precisely this narrowness was desirable. He even underlined it, by compressing the space even more, and through this very method achieved a previously unimagined monumentality. The area of the fight between David and the powerful, already prone giant is diminished by a tent rising in the background. Judith and her maid tremble, as if over an abyss, on a very small base; and the three-part story of Esther, with Haman hanging in the middle, takes place shoved into an astonishingly reduced space. This method of narrowing the space and compressing the bodies, so contrary to the breadth and the comfortably organized arrangements of classical feeling, reaches an expression of even greater strength and vitality in a representation of a mass action like the *Brazen Serpent*. For these reasons this heroic composition might be called the first painting of the mannerist line, though it lacks the special stiffness of later development (of Bronzino, for example, who treated the theme in imitation of Michelangelo, but at the same time with characteristic differences). Actually, construction is given solely by means of figures which press up against each other and push each other—the row of the faithful on the left, and the larger group of the unfaithful on the right caught in the twinings of the serpent. Only in the middle and far in the background is a break opened up, in which the upright image of the brazen serpent appears against a bright light. To be sure, through this means a view into depth is provided, but this isolated breakthrough does not prevent the feeling of spacelessness or narrowing of space. The tense, the breathless, is forced by the piling up of powerful bodies in very great motion, torn by layers of light in a space inadequate for them, so that one might fear lest the intertwined limbs spill over and burst from the frame to left and right. The same is true of the *Last Judgment,* the work of Michelangelo's later period which overwhelmed everything else simply by its dimensions and by the intensity of its gestures, and which produced a mixture of terror and admiration. Here too an effect of depth is present, called forth by the naked rock barrier in the front, which allows the eye a point of departure because it is the one solid point in the whole painting, as well as by the bark of Charon at the top, and by the circular vortex with the Jupiter-Christ figure at its center. A space, then, is present, but this space is not an optical one, such as in Rubens' *Fall of the Angels,* leaving the gleaming nude figures bathed in light and air, nor is it an organized tactile one in which well-constructed individuals and well-balanced groups live and expand. Rather it is a space without reality, without existence, in its upper section completely filled with human bodies, which, tied up in bunches, come loose and descend from the whole, and when seen from a distance float about like wisps of cloud. Here too optical and spatial elements are present—the pushing in and out of forms, the light with its contrasts and its divisions of groups; but the very lack of a unified viewpoint prevents any illusionistic effect, as does likewise the relative scale, impossible from an optical standpoint, of the unforeshortened upper figures and the lower, which ought to be much larger. Already in the seventeenth century Francesco Albani objected to this. Even predominantly "haptic," that is, tangible elements are undeniable; these are found in the symmetrical arrangement and unification of the main upper group, and especially in the thorough execution of the plastic and the corporeal, whose unprecedented mastery early brought forth unrestrained admiration of Michelangelo's knowledge of anatomy. But these too are canceled out, first through the completely unhaptic pushing together and merging of the figures within the sections, and the piling up of bodies, and second through the exaggeration of the modeling in single figures through the "wave-swell thrust of musculature" (which is no doubt what Annibale Carracci meant when in contrast to the figures of the Sistine Ceiling he characterized the nudes of the *Last Judgment* as too anatomical). Similar disapproval was brought up against the equalization of bodily forms in young and old, and in men and women, resulting in a certain schematism. All this—the unreal and unconstructed space, the building up of the bodily volumes, especially the whole overwhelming predominance of the body, especially the nude, and finally the powerful emphasis of the anatomical at the expense of the normal and the proportioned—all these things made the *Last Judgment* the principal work of the anticlassic mannerist artistic attitude, surpassing all else in spiritual depth and formal construction.

The Cappella Paolina frescoes, done during the forties, exist like Michelangelo's late versions of the Pietà, in an heroic isolation. The space has become more starkly unreal than in the *Last Judgment.* There are, to be sure, certain allusions to depth—the arms of the cross of Peter, the horse dashing off backwards in the *Conversion of St. Paul,* and so on—and even foreshortening is not neglected, as in the figure of Christ leaning down and forward. However, structure is manifested only through bodily volumes. In comparison with them the hilltops indicated in the background have no existence; neither through perspective, nor in terms of figure sizes and relations is anything like a Renaissance view into the distance set up. (In the *Crucifixion of St. Peter,* for example, the group of figures of women cut off by the edge is much too small.) The figures are even more abstractly but also more strongly linked together than in the *Last Judgment* (which is similar in its general arrangement). This is so not only because of an ornamental linkage established through common movements or opposing movements, though these too are very conspicuous, but even more because of vital tensions which, running through the volumes of the bodies and attaching them to each other, tie them together in groups, or separate and isolate them. Thus in this work—typical of an "old-age style"—Michelangelo had reached a pitch of spiritual abstraction that was scarcely understood. So these frescoes, which because they are in a private chapel were difficult of access to the profane eye, have had no important influence.[8]

And yet Michelangelo expressed a powerful idea with typically mannerist methods in a period when Mannerism in central Italy already had become partly decorative and empty. Only one other

[8] Taddeo Zuccaro took over a figure from the *Conversion of St. Paul* in his painting in the Doria Gallery. The frescoes must have been made available to him, since the ceiling in the Pauline Chapel was executed by the Zuccari.

man in Italy still held this idea aloft, and this was Tintoretto, a kindred spirit not unmoved by Michelangelo.

It is notable that the direct circle of Michelangelo's followers, more particularly Sebastiano del Piombo and Daniele da Volterra (we may exclude Venusti), did not significantly carry forward these anticlassical tendencies of the master. Their work, to be sure, exhibits some features of Mannerism, which, in any case, after 1520 few artists could altogether escape. One can discover its traces even within the school of Raphael which, from the later stanza on, does not take up the Baroque of the Heliodorus in any effective way but, manneristically, becomes much more unoptical and unspatial. In Giulio Romano (who becomes of extraordinary importance for the classicism of the seventeenth century) this is the case. Even more striking is the changeable Baldassare Peruzzi, who evolves from his *quattrocento*-like works (St. Onofrio), to the high classical ones (*Presentation in the Temple* in Santa Maria della Pace), and finally in his late period around 1530, definitively goes over to Mannerism (*Augustus and the Sibyl* in Siena). Often too the boundary lines between the more classicizing and the manneristic manner are hazy. In any case, neither Sebastiano nor Daniele has any influence upon the early period of Mannerism.

This is shown very clearly by the way in which Daniele in his famous *Crucifixion* in San Pietro Montorio treats the subject in a quite different and haptic way than did Rosso in his significant early *Crucifixion*.

The new anticlassical style, which was later condescendingly labeled "the manneristic," is not (as in times past people were fond of saying) merely a minor variety of Michelangelo's great art; nor is it merely a misunderstood exaggeration, or a weak and empty flattening of prototypes of the master into a mannered journeyman's or arts-and-crafts manner. It is instead a style which, as part of a movement purely spiritual in origin, from the start turned specifically against a certain superficiality that exuded from an all too balanced and beautiful classic art, and thus embraced Michelangelo as its greatest exponent but which in an important area remained independent of him (and only in one of its later currents clung to him in a definite and conscious way).

In his *Visitation* of 1516 (Fig. 1) Pontormo remains on the whole within the patterns of his master, Andrea del Sarto. The soft colors, which Pontormo perhaps applies somewhat more strongly, the strong volumetric stance of the figures, the ideal stage space that does not reach very far back into depth, closed by the optically effective semicircular niche, and softly shadowed (in Fra Bartolommeo's way)—this is a continuation of the style of Andrea del Sarto and is of a high quality. This painting of Pontormo represents Florentine classicism at its most brilliant. One can appreciate Vasari's account of the public impressiveness of a painting so balanced and so beautiful in color. It is, precisely, a splendid example of tectonic structure and well-weighted compositional organization. All the more understandable, therefore, is Vasari's astonishment that a man of Pontormo's quality should give up the achievements of his study—this much admired clarity and beauty —and brusquely attach himself to a completely opposite tendency. "One must plainly feel sympathy with a man so foolish as to slough off his good former manner which pleased everyone exceptionally well, and was much better than all others, and with incredible effort seek to pursue something which others avoid or try to forget. Did not Pontormo know that Germans and Flemings come to us in order to learn the Italian manner which he gave up as if it were worthless?"

A transition is provided by the *Madonna and Child with Saints* (1518) in San Michele Visdomini (Fig. 2).[9] The niche architecture, while still present, is no longer the same empty background

[9] Occasionally a replica in the former Doetsch collection has been considered the original, but to the contrary see Carlo Gamba, *I disegni di J. Carrucci detto il Pontormo* (Florence, 1912), and Piccola Collezione d'Arte, No. 15.

foil built up tectonically so as to widen the space in a beautiful curve. Instead, it is almost completely hidden by the volumes of the bodies and really functions only as a rather strongly shadowed cloak for the Madonna. The pyramidal triangle is still the old standardized schema,[10] but the balance, the arrangement of weights is destroyed. The Madonna's head forms the point of the triangle but the axis of her body, which formerly would have been in the middle, is pushed slightly toward the right, destroying the isosceles triangle.

Thus the whole painting acquires a swing to the right and into depth, which is further enhanced by light and shade and is only canceled out by the counteraction of the three parallel diagonals that keep the central composition from getting completely out of order.[11] The figures too are shoved in upon each other much more recklessly; the space is thus narrowed in comparison to the earlier, more broadly settled composition. These are all outspoken unacademic displacements, but Renaissance elements are still very strongly present. The execution of the figures is still plastic and grows outward from an internal center, following the style Leonardo had created and Andrea del Sarto had in part adopted. In the facial expressions as well, especially that of the Madonna, an echo of the Leonardesque smile seems to remain. The chiaroscuro, which Pontormo otherwise utilizes very little, may come also from this source, but it is rougher than in Leonardo and also exceeds the light and shade of Andrea del Sarto, which, for example in his *Marriage of St. Catherine,* is much more *sfumato.* From the sharpness of the gestures, from the movement in a circle and in depth, one might infer with equal justice a tendency either toward the Baroque or toward Mannerism. One might think the composition was a prank of a young painter who had had quite enough of the

[10] As it is to some extent in Andrea del Sarto's *Marriage of St. Catherine,* of about 1512, which it much recalls in the arrangement.

[11] The same thing is also to be seen turning up in Giulio Romano in his *Anima* painting, later in date.

colorful beauty of Andrea del Sarto, and the healthy balance of
Albertinelli and Fra Bartolommeo, and who for once wanted to
try out something different and freer. A strong swing of the com-
pass is evident but just where it will come to rest is not quite clear.
All this is documented also by the charming lunette decorations in
Poggio a Caiano (ca. 1520 to 1521, Fig. 3) with the figures of
Vertumnus and Pomona—a creation of half-playful grace such as
one would never have expected from the painter of the very serious
Visdomini picture. How casual and apparently carefree—though
closer observation reveals a very tight ornamental structure—are
the light figures strewn around both sides of the round window
opening, and given bounds and limits by a low wall. The three
figures of women on the right side are almost as graceful as the
Rococo. This fresco in its lovable grace and happy tone seems still
far removed from the new style which develops, in Pontormo
particularly, so seriously and without a backward look. Only the
very narrow layer of space, within which the figures, for all their
contraposto and strong movements, are held, indicates the new
vision.

How almost the same composition looks when it is transposed to
an anticlassical style is shown by the broadly sketched drawing in
the Uffizi (Fig. 4).[12] It has become winter; there is the same round
window opening as in the executed fresco, but around it, instead of

[12] No. 454, Bernard Berenson, *Drawings of the Florentine Painters* (London,
1903 and Chicago, 1938), I, 311, proposes that this drawing, stylistically so different, is about ten to twelve years later than the fresco, i.e., at the beginning of
the thirties when Pontormo, who had not completed the work in Poggio a
Caiano, received a commission for it for the second time. However, Mortimer
Clapp, *Les Dessins de Pontormo* (Paris, 1914) considers the drawing to be for a
variant project from the same period as the fresco. In that case the stylistic vari-
ability of the artist would be astonishing. The drawing of the figures is surely
after 1530, when Pontormo had temporarily come strongly under Michelangelo's
influence. On the other hand, the Uffizi drawing departs too greatly from the
fresco even in content to be merely a variant. Conceivably it is a project for another lunette (like Uffizi No. 455) which comes before 1530 but later than the
fresco.

softly leaning bodies beautifully covered with leaves twine bare, hard, knotty limbs. Here too there are three figures on each side—the *putti* are canceled out as too playful—but they no longer have a comfortable space for their development. Tangled in the empty branches, holding tightly on to them, they are ornamentally inter-twined—their volumes fill the corners of the lunettes and through their plasticity build the space which is otherwise not indicated, thus producing an anticlassical, manneristic crowding of decoration which is completely opposed to the composition as executed. Psychologically, too, there is a strong contrast, for these are wild figures: four naked men and only two women whose outstretched, twisted limbs cut past each other within the narrow space. A severe monumentality has taken the place of the sixteenth-century grace of the fresco. It is, therefore, very likely that this drawing is not a preparatory study but was produced later than the fresco at Poggio a Caiano.[13]

Immediately after this exceedingly graceful decorative piece for the Medici Villa, there follows the breakthrough to the new style, as seen in the surprising and almost shocking frescoes for the Certosa (1522 to 1525). Painted, as Vasari reports, when Pontormo had fled from the plague to the remote Certosa in the Valdema, these consist of five scenes from the Passion executed on the walls of the transept. As if impelled by the tragedy of the theme toward an-

[13] The preference for *contraposti* could, to be sure, derive from Michelangelo's formal language, at least in a quite general way, i.e., from the art of Michelangelo when he was still more or less close to nature (e.g., the *Battle of Cascina*). Drawings of Pontormo also refer back to it. It would be more interesting to know whether at that stage of his activity Pontormo already knew the Sistine. The nude youth sitting on the wall who grasps the branch as it leans down, recalls the Jonas in its backward strain. (Observation by Panofsky.) Yet it is precisely the characteristic element which is lacking—the strong foreshortening. Assuming that Pontormo thought of the extraordinary figure of the Prophet at all, it would mean that the wild giant limbs had been transformed into something easy, almost graceful. Drawings made from the Sistine may also have been available to Pontormo. Michelangelo himself, who at about this time lived in Florence, seems first to have come into closer contact with Pontormo at a later period.

other and more inward style, Pontormo has shed all that was graceful and shining in the Renaissance atmosphere. All that had been
established by Andrea del Sarto and his circle, the emphasis on the
plastic and the bodily, the material and coloristic, the realized space
and the all too blooming flesh tones—everything outward now
disappears. In its place are a formal and psychological simplifica-
tion, a rhythm, a subdued but still beautiful coloring (with fewer
hues and nuances than Andrea del Sarto preferred), and above all
an expression rising from the depth of the soul and hitherto un-
known in this age and style.

In a *Christ Before Pilate* (Fig. 5), the figure of Christ, his hands
tied to his back, is turned to the side so that his silhouette is a thin,
Gothically swung curve. He is dressed in light violet, a delicate,
fragile, and transparent figure standing before Pilate, enthroned
at one side, in the midst of his attackers and surrounded by armed
men. All these men are schematic, unplastic, posed in an unreal
space. Two halberdiers in white armor rise ghostly and bodiless
into the painting to mark the frontal boundary of the space. It is
cut off at the back by a terrace, while a servant, seen from quite
another angle of vision, descends the steps with a golden pitcher
and bowl.

Likewise formally simplified and inward in a northern sense is
the *Pietà* (Fig. 6) unfortunately badly damaged, as are also the
Carrying of the Cross and the *Gethsemane*. The great vertical of
the posts and ladders of the background underlines the stiffness of
the upright figures of the mourners, placed before the diagonally
set body so that they are seen head on. Here the question of a balanced composition in the Renaissance sense, or of a movement of
centered figures in free space no longer arises. Archaically rough,
simple vessels of feeling, these almost bodiless figures stand beyond
reality. This spirituality comes to light most purely in the *Resurrection* (Fig. 7). Here Christ, his outstretched body swathed in a
whitish burial robe, floats upward. The sleeping soldiers crouch on
the ground at both sides, while their rising spears mark the vertical.
Here too, especially in the body of Christ, there is to be observed a

spiritualization whose ethereal and ecstatic form, utterly opposed to the healthy Renaissance ideal, is to grow gradually in the later *cinquecento* until it reaches El Greco. Toward this spirituality all the formal achievements of Renaissance art in spatial organization and exact placement of figures is intentionally discarded. And this in turn gives rise to the feeling of the primitive, a style that, compared to the fully conscious and mastered style of the Renaissance, is consciously retrospective.

It is no wonder that in Florence these paintings, so differently articulated from the usual ones, inevitably, like everything new, stimulated a great and naturally painful attention. Vasari expresses this clearly in the passages from his biography of Pontormo which we have cited at the outset; and he also shows what it was that must have disturbed the Italians in this new and surprising art—the unsensual and its connection with heightened spiritual expression—in a word, the Gothic. It was precisely the Gothic which the Renaissance, insofar as it felt itself the heir of antiquity, had most bitterly fought, for the Gothic was the symptom of decline in art, the tasteless and the barbaric. Yet this northern element kept turning up again and again, and Albrecht Dürer, however much he was himself nourished by Renaissance materials, was marveled at and exploited at the beginning of the Renaissance as the most brilliant exemplar of the northern spirit. Now it is highly characteristic that Pontormo, as one of the pioneers of the new anticlassic rhythmical style, disgusted by the formalism of the Florentine High Renaissance, should take the psychic stance of the German master to himself during his flight to the Valdema, and even enhance its spiritual meaning. There was no need for the large shipment of Dürer prints, which has been mentioned, to make Pontormo aware of the German master. He had already seen Andrea del Sarto utilize Dürer's engravings and woodcuts in his compositions, as he did those of Schongauer. But Andrea del Sarto limits himself essentially to taking over isolated elements;[14] rarely does he absorb

---

[14] As, for example, the man at the extreme right in the *Beheading of John* in the Scalzo from Dürer (see Bartsch 10 and elsewhere).

any of Dürer's spatial relationships. His relations stop at externals; no spiritual deepening, no deeply probing alteration of the Renaissance interpretation occurs. Such borrowings the public or Vasari might have pardoned in the artist, or might perchance even have welcomed, but Pontormo did not merely appropriate externals from Dürer; he went further and deeper—for him Dürer was the expression and symbol of his own revolutionary anticlassical point of view. Hence he read much into Dürer and drew much from him —precisely the secret Gothic element which Dürer himself set out to overcome, and this core he took and rearranged in his own way. The remarkable phenomenon is that Pontormo, still a Renaissance artist as to period, in imitating the late Gothic German artist became more archaic and more Gothic than his prototype.

The seated sleeping figure at the left in the *Resurrection* is taken from the small woodcut *Passion* of Dürer, and the figure of the Saviour clearly goes back to the Resurrected figure of the *Great Passion*. Not only the outward stance and gesture of the figures, but virtually their dynamic function in the whole image are taken over by Pontormo from Dürer, but out of the country bumpkin of Dürer has grown a sort of cavalier with an almost too elegant expression. Above all, though, the figure of Christ has changed surprisingly. Dürer's robust male figure, executed in a thoroughly anatomical way, has in Pontormo turned into a swaying, supernaturally elongated figure.[15] All that is physical whether in Andrea del Sarto's or Dürer's sense, has vanished—there remains only the delicate, bright, almost bodiless appearance, completely transformed into spirit, which sweeps upward in a spaceless existence. The overrefinement of the lines goes hand in hand in Pontormo with a

[15] This comes out even more clearly in a Berlin drawing, which rises up more narrowly and steeply. Conceivably it is not autograph, though, but made after Pontormo. Cf. Fritz Goldschmidt, "Frederick Mortimer Clapp. On Certain Drawings of Pontormo" in *Repertorium für Kunstwissenschaft*, 35 (1912), 559; "Kupferstichkabinet Zeichningen von Jacopo Carucci da Pontormo" in *Amtliche Berichte aus den preussischen Kunstsammlungen*, 36 (1914-15), 84; and Hermann Voss, *Die Malerei der Spaetrenaissance in Rom und Florenz* (Berlin, 1920), p. 169.

slightly neurotic sensibility of expression, not found in the serene Sarto, but which, consistent with the more strongly dematerialized space, goes back beyond Dürer almost into the *trecento* manner. It is also interesting to note how in the *Christ Before Pilate,* Pontormo introduces the halberdiers, seen from the back and cut off in the foreground. It is probable that Dürer's seated half-figures in the *Bathhouse,* which are similarly cut off by a sharp railing, gave Pontormo the stimulus, but how completely they differ from Dürer in their bodily plasticity and their suggestion of space. In Pontormo they move into the painting seen strictly from the back, pane-like, almost without any deepening of space into the picture plane, conceived as *repoussoir* figures as in Dürer, but only in terms of a very slight, practically unreal, spatial layer. But precisely through these means the uncorporeal and soulful aspect of the swaying Christ figure between them comes more insistently to our consciousness. These figures seen from the back carry the picture away from the beholder, make it more unreal and more distant. This too is an anticlassical motif, which turns up for the first time in Mannerism and is expanded from there on.[16]

Thus Pontormo's contact with the northern Gothic produces the spark needed for a radical change of his style. The disposition had long been present in him—he had already given warning of his desire for a revolt in the almost willful shifts from the norm in the painting of 1518 in San Michele.[17] Above and beyond this individ-

[16] In Andrea del Sarto such half figures in the foreground, half or completely turned toward the spectator, link him up with the holy event in a quite opposite way—thus it becomes a subjective and Baroque motif (e.g., in the *Madonna with Saints* of the Kaiser Friedrich Museum, 1528). Figures seen from the back in the sense of Pontormo (his are the earliest) appear on the other hand in El Greco, for example in the *Spoiling of Christ.*

[17] But likewise too in other paintings which cannot be more thoroughly treated here, for example in the *cassoni* from the *Life of Joseph* at Panshanger and in the National Gallery in London, the last of which is striking through its quite exceptionally abstruse arrangement of space and proportion of the figures. Most remarkable, too, is the *John the Evangelist* at Pontormo (Pieve) which, in its long, lanky figure of an aged man, recalls El Greco, and which was created re-

ual tendency, however, Pontormo's ability to absorb and transmute foreign materials into something new, and so depart completely from what had preceded him, was part of a new stylistic urge which lay dormant in others as well. It emerged at the same time (the beginning of the twenties) in the works of a few other fore-runners, these men too pioneers of a new art which was soon to dominate the old.

Closely akin to Pontormo is Rosso Fiorentino who now, though with some hesitation, accomplishes the break with the Renaissance, with the all too balanced Fra Bartolommeo and the all too beautiful and soft Andrea del Sarto. His earliest work, the *Assumption* (Fig. 8) of about 1515 to 1516, in the forecourt of the Annunziata, already shows a great independence of will when compared with the other frescoes done there by Andrea del Sarto, and Francia-bigio, but it also differs from Pontormo. The beautiful coloring of Andrea del Sarto, the fine painterly flow of tones (*unione*) which Pontormo himself never completely renounced, has given way to an impetuous application of colors. Strong red and yellow, then green, are set beside each other with scarcely a transition; violet tones, golden clouds, dominate in the upper portions. The drawing is less exact, dimmer, especially in the faces; on the other hand the closely massed apostles in the lower part of the picture overlap like a wall, so that though the figures are conceived in a plastic, spatial manner, there remains little room for recession in depth. The compact mass reminds us of the cluster of apostles in Titian's *Assumption* (painted just a little later), in which the moment of exodus is much more emphasized, breaking an unornamental path into the background through optical as well as plastic effects and destroying the rigidity. On the other hand, Rosso con-fronts us in the *Gloria* with a pure illusionistic motif. Here a Ma-donna figure, quite clearly recalling Fra Bartolommeo, is sur-

---

markably early, about 1517 (according to Gamba, *Disegni,* p. 5). It would be tempting to place it rather in the neighborhood of the stiffly soaring Louvre composition of the *Holy Family.*

rounded by *putti* which, foreshortened and standing on their heads, already anticipate Correggio. It is equally bold of Rosso to let the hem of the middle apostle fall out over the frame, contrary to every Renaissance feeling. Thus quite early Rosso exhibits a clear tendency to burst the canonical bonds, even if he achieves no radical reversal. On the whole there can often be determined in Rosso a wavering between the old and the new. His *Madonna Enthroned with Saints* in the Uffizi is still generally constructed as a niche composition, entirely within the stylistic framework of the Florentine High Renaissance. The bodily structure, and modeling too, are not divergent in principle from Andrea del Sarto's, but the handling of the surfaces is quite different. Color and light are emphasized with extraordinarily greater sharpness, and become cruder and harsher. Everything is depicted in heavy accents—the green in the foreground, the changing tones in the sleeves of the kneeling figures, the sharp light which falls on the ravaged face of the greybeard at the left; the poisonous tones that Andrea del Sarto had always avoided now appear; the faces are more common although, or perhaps, because, something overly sweet predominates in them. The large *Marriage of the Virgin* in San Lorenzo (1523, Fig. 9) is a more imposing picture in which the new tendency makes its clear appearance. The arrangement of the figures on the steps, with the priest as the central figure, is not so surprising, but essentially the space is formed through the mass of figures thickly pressed against each other and disappears into the background toward the church door in a layer intentionally left indefinite. The figures themselves, especially in this main group, are very strongly elongated, so that verticalism dominates throughout this work. The color again betrays strong luministic tendencies.

But the work in which Rosso takes the decisive step away from the balanced and classical towards the spiritual and subjective is the 1521 *Deposition from the Cross* in Volterra (Fig. 10). This picture embodies essentially the same attitude we have already met in Pontormo's frescoes at the Certosa, even if it is somewhat differently oriented because of Rosso's very different artistic temperament—a conscious reversal and a return to a kind of primitivism, if one may use this expression, in contradistinction to the universally developed and mature Renaissance feeling. In this respect the painting recalls the medieval Gothic, without its being proper to seek for a definite prototype not even in Sienese art. One might say here too that the "latent Gothic" which lived on in the *quattrocento* style of Castagno or Uccello or Tura (for this often misused slogan has its justification here) bursts its bonds in this most beautiful creation of Rosso partly prompted, no doubt, by a certain revulsion toward the feeling of some of his own compositions in which the Andrea del Sarto style had merely been made wilder. Along with this, the movements in Rosso's painting function in a way that is more refined, more precious, more artistic—in a word, manneristic. If one compares it with the *Deposition from the Cross* by Filippino Lippi (completed by Perugino at the beginning of the *cinquecento*), which in its general structure was the prototype for Rosso's picture, then one will feel the uncommonly acute difference. This is no simple continuation of the theme, such as one may discover in Daniele da Volterra's great painting,[18] but a reworking into a quite different kind of feeling. Even though Rosso took over the theme of the two ladders, he was still able to make out of this motif, with its direct requirement of stability, something at once vertical and swaying, simply through the very high and narrow format in which he composed the whole. These ladders serve as a weak armature for a wreath of figures which twine rhythmically in and out among each other. Some of the proportions are extraordinarily elongated—the moving figure of John, for example, who, hiding his face in his hands, bends over and turns away weeping, with a detachment which recalls El Greco. The space is unreal throughout; the figures hardly fill it up,

[18] Daniele must have known Rosso's painting in Volterra, but in contrast to Voss, *Spätrenaissance*, p. 123, I would also assume a direct link, especially in the upper group, with the *Crucifixion* of Filippino in the Academy.

but stand in front of it like ghosts. The sharp light, the peculiarly shining colors, the curves of their long outstretched limbs, bestow on these figures something unreal, far removed from any ideal canon. It is absolutely amazing how, occasionally, volumes of bodies are constructed cubically out of surfaces which, lighted in various ways, meet each other with sharp angles. This is especially striking in the kneeling Magdalen who embraces the knee of the Mater Dolorosa. As in Pontormo, but even more passionately, with more accentuation and richer light and color, this suppression of the usual and the balanced leads to a new spirituality, an astonishing soulful expressiveness, which even Rosso himself rarely reaches again. Gesture, become too rhetorical during the Renaissance, now acquires a new meaning, pointed (almost caricatural) in its sharpness and expressive through its stylization. The figure of the old man above the body of Christ is nothing new in itself, but the way it leans on the crosspiece with both arms and, with its unkempt Chronos-head and its fluttering mantle, looms over the cross to form a lunette that crowns the whole, has in it something entirely unique and unprecedented. The same thing applies to the lower figures. Everything is heightened, and everything that would disturb or diminish this heightening—space, perspective, mass, normal proportion—is left out or transformed. A general influence from Michelangelo is difficult to determine; the greater inwardness which runs through the movement is perhaps related to him. In the figure of the Saviour, however, a detailed relation does exist. The expression of the head, its diagonal position seen from below, the posture of the arm, as of the whole body, is doubtless to be derived directly from the stretched out figure of Christ in Michelangelo's *Pietà* group, and the dying slave also has a certain connection with it. Yet Rosso was no more really permeated by Michelangelo's influence than Pontormo was when he made use of motifs from the battle cartoon. Any direct northern influence (in any case very much slighter than with Pontormo) is hardly ascertainable; to be sure, the reaction of the late Gothic against the classical which does turn up at the same time in the north (e.g., Cranach) is similar in spirit, but its appearance in Italy is naturally much more surprising.

Rosso's very remarkable painting which now hangs in the Tribuna of the Uffizi, *Moses Defending the Daughters of Jethro* (Fig. 11) is not formulated in terms of psychic depth, but is built on a purely esthetic basis of form, color, ornamental overlapping, and spatial layers, yet it is very characteristic of the new interpretation. It must have been executed before 1523, for about this time Rosso left Florence and went to Rome. The Michelangelesque influence extends only to the foreshortened nude figures of the stricken shepherds in the foreground who very clearly betray a study of the *Bathing Soldiers*. Moses, like them, foreshortened, almost entirely nude, with blond hair flying and blond beard, exhibits a stronger and even wilder *contrapposto* than his prototype in the engravings by Agostino Veneziano. He stands behind or above the figures which have been struck down and is striking a third, while a fourth on the other side, with a very red face and similar light blond locks, his mouth wide open, shouts out of the picture. Even further upward a new attacker, shadowy in contrast with the bright bodies down below, a flying mantle as a circular foil at his side, storms in from the side toward a girl. She is surrounded by the frightened lambs, her arm outstretched in fright, a light cloak around her otherwise exposed body, sheer astonishment on her pretty face. At the extreme upper edge of the picture, behind a railing, are to be seen fleeing girls, buildings, and two overlapping profiles. Multiplied layers, brutally projected gestures, strong plastic volumes of bodies which, pressed closely together, leave hardly a single unfilled patch of surface anywhere, strong but entirely unreal colors, characterize this painting, for which the entire Renaissance furnishes no prototype. A feeling of space, of a certain depth, does arise through the "addition of layers" set behind or above each other. Apart from the bodies, each of which builds its own spatial volume, there is no indication of depth through perspective. Instead of this, parallel layers move with the surface of the painting, a step marking the first third and a railing the second. Even the figure storming in from the side moves parallel to the picture plane, and the movement of Moses functions in a similar way. The extreme plasticity of the single figures is thus, as a whole, absorbed into the two-dimensional quality of the picture surface and so subdued, although a certain realistic effect of depth in space is maintained through the actual spatial volumes and the succession of layers. The unstable tension between the picture surface and the effect of depth thus created, combined with an interlocking of layers, is a typical manneristic method.[19] Rosso's picture is indeed the earliest in which this kind of spatial organization is presented in its extreme form. Since Rosso is altogether a stronger colorist than the other Florentine mannerists, he employs light and color to a striking extent in order to achieve this layer structure. The layer in the foreground, brightly lighted, has a green base against which are set off the light yellow bodies and the red-brown wild hair. Higher, beyond the step, there is a bluish layer, somewhat more in shadow, out of which shine the red hair of Moses and his red garment. The darkly shaded striding man with his flying, poisonous violet garment and the light blue of the girl are set above this. With the red-brown of the railing begins the narrowest, highest layer where red, yellow, and green light up in the garments of the fleeing figures and a piece of the sky shows between yellow-brown houses. In contrast with the other paintings of Rosso, the proportions of the single figures are not especially elongated; the masses of the bodies of the daughters of Jethro are almost standard. In spite of this through the compressed piling up within the tall format there does arise a feeling of verticalism thoroughly expressive of the new style. Al-

[19] Compare, for example, the allegory by Bronzino in London. This "addition of the layers" thus pushes on into the classicistic too (compare my book *Nicolas Poussin* [Munich, 1914]); only the shuttling back and forth disappears.

together, in both construction and color, this painting of Rosso's is the strangest, wildest picture created in the whole period, and stands quite apart from every canonical normative feeling.[20]

THE third among the creators and prototypes of the anticlassical mannerist style is not a Florentine but a north Italian. This is Francesco Parmigianino, born in 1503, and thus almost a decade younger than Pontormo and Rosso. Furthermore, he stems from a basically different artistic culture and thus contributes a different artistic pattern. For he did not have to struggle against the stability of Roman and Florentine High Renaissance art, and he had not, in his youth, absorbed like mother's milk the plastic anatomy of the bathing soldiers of Michelangelo. For him instead the grace and the optical subjectivism of Correggio had been the source in his decisive years, and he was himself inclined by his whole nature to increase and refine the delicacy and the courtly elegance of his master. Thus the transition to the new style is not nearly so rough and revolutionary in him as in the two Florentines. With these limitations in mind, one can say that the relation of the developed art of Parmigianino to Correggio is in general the same as that of Pontormo and Rosso to Andrea del Sarto and the Florentine High Renaissance.

The early works in Parma show the style of Correggio—the *Marriage of St. Catherine* in the Gallery of Parma, for example, is put together out of Correggesque motifs. More interesting are the niche figures in San Giovanni Evangelista which, though their prototype in spatial organization and construction of masses is Correggio's handsome lunette of St. John on Patmos in the same church, nevertheless already show a great individuality. For even more than in Correggio's *St. John* the figures fill the space of the

[20] One may compare with this the handling of the same theme by Botticelli in the Sistine Chapel in order to recognize the difference between a "Gothic artist of the early Renaissance" and an early mannerist.

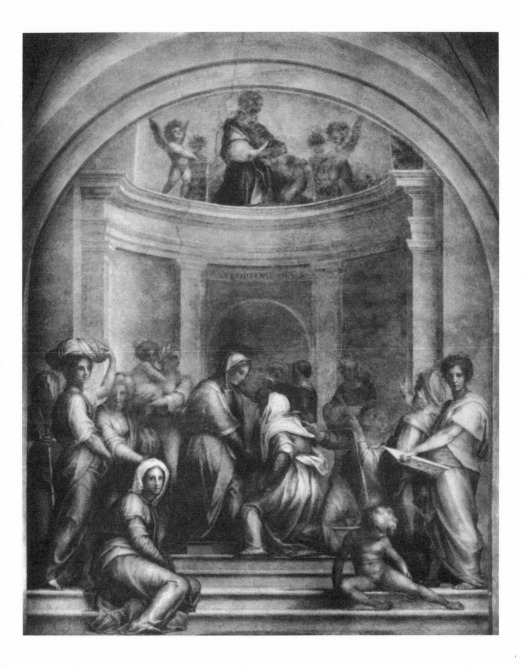

1 JACOPO PONTORMO: VISITATION. FLORENCE, CHIOSTRO DELL'ANNUNZIATA

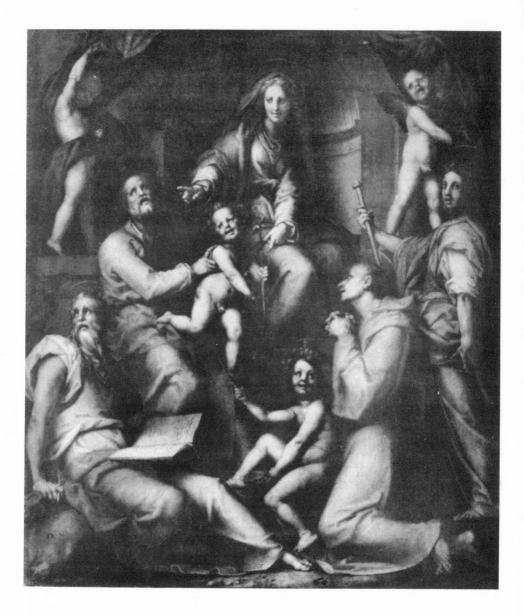

2   JACOPO PONTORMO: MADONNA AND CHILD WITH SAINTS. FLORENCE, S. MICHELE VISDOMINI

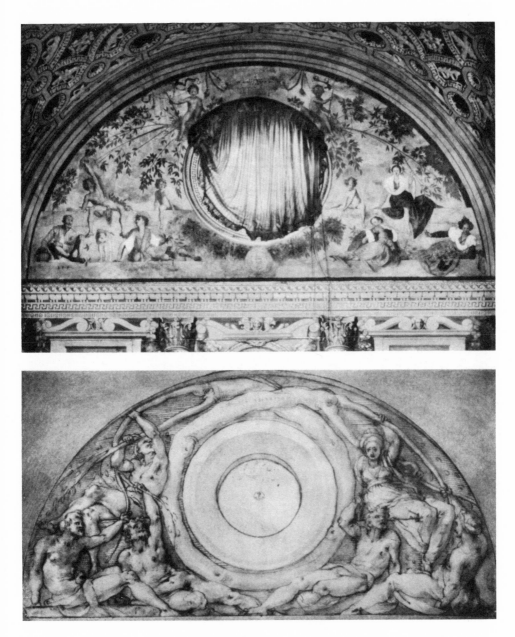

3 JACOPO PONTORMO: VERTUMNUS AND POMONA. FLORENCE, POGGIO A CAIANO

4 JACOPO PONTORMO: STUDY FOR LUNETTE DECORATION AT POGGIO A CAIANO. FLORENCE, UFFIZI

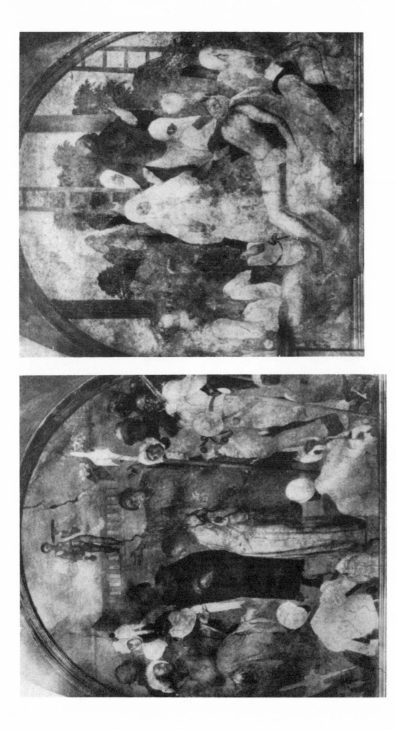

5 JACOPO PONTORMO: CHRIST BEFORE PILATE. FLORENCE, CERTOSA DEL GALLUZZO

6 JACOPO PONTORMO: PIETÀ. FLORENCE, CERTOSA DEL GALLUZZO

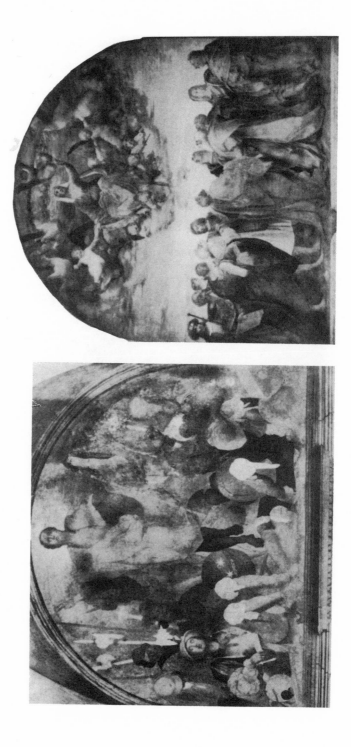

7 JACOPO PONTORMO: RESURRECTION. FLORENCE, CERTOSA DEL GALLUZZO

8 ROSSO FIORENTINO: ASSUMPTION OF THE VIRGIN. FLORENCE, SS. ANNUNZIATA

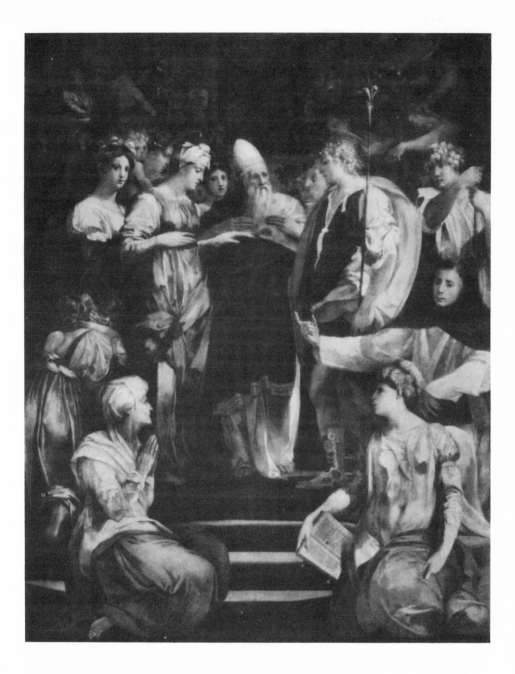

9 ROSSO FIORENTINO: MARRIAGE OF THE VIRGIN. FLORENCE, S. LORENZO

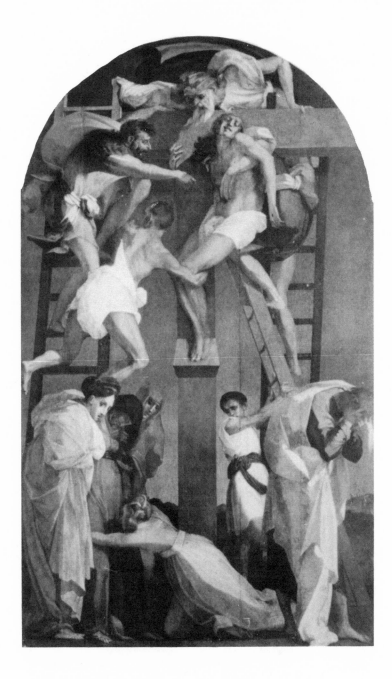

10 ROSSO FIORENTINO: DEPOSITION FROM THE CROSS. VOLTERRA, PINACOTECA

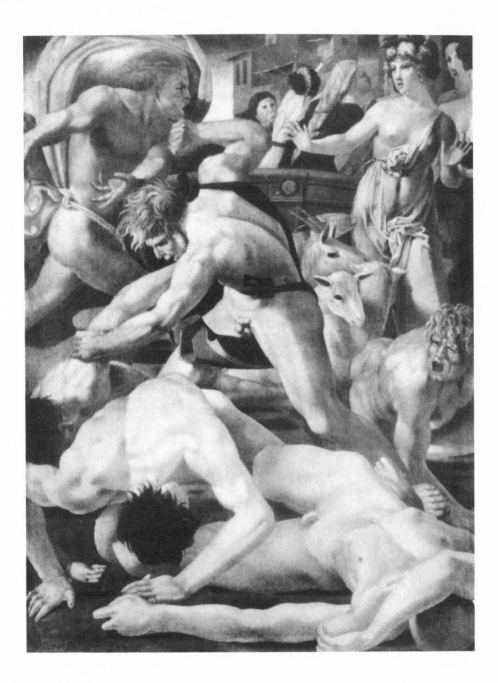

11 ROSSO FIORENTINO: MOSES AND THE DAUGHTERS OF JETHRO. FLORENCE, UFFIZI

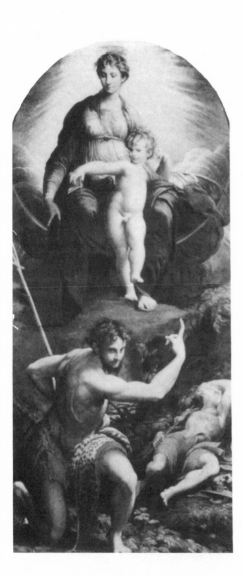

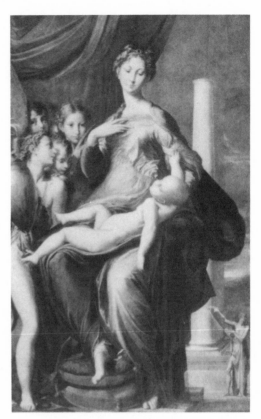

12 PARMIGIANINO: VISION OF ST. JEROME. LONDON, NATIONAL GALLERY

13 PARMIGIANINO: MADONNA DAL COLLO LUNGO. FLORENCE, PITTI

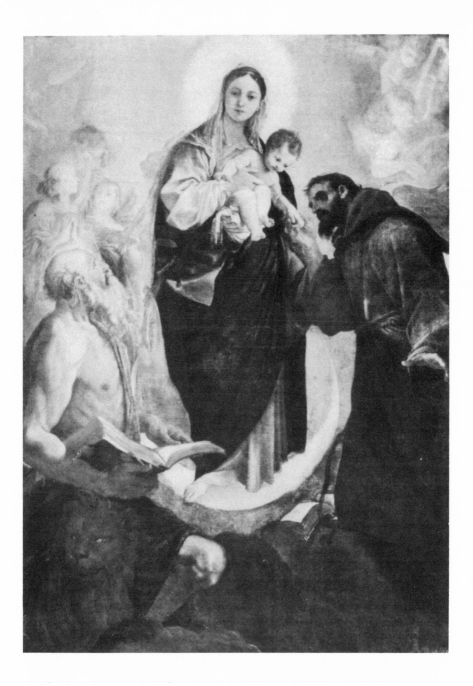

14 LODOVICO CARRACCI: MADONNA DEGLI SCALZI. BOLOGNA, PINACOTECA

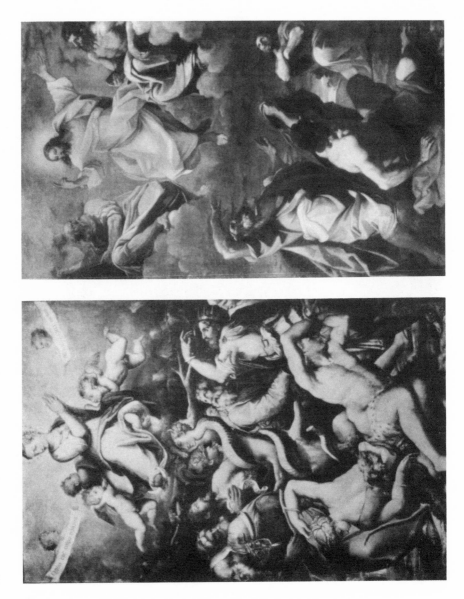

15 GIORGIO VASARI: IMMACULATE CONCEPTION. LUCCA, PINACOTECA

16 LODOVICO CARRACCI: TRANSFIGURATION. BOLOGNA, PINACOTECA

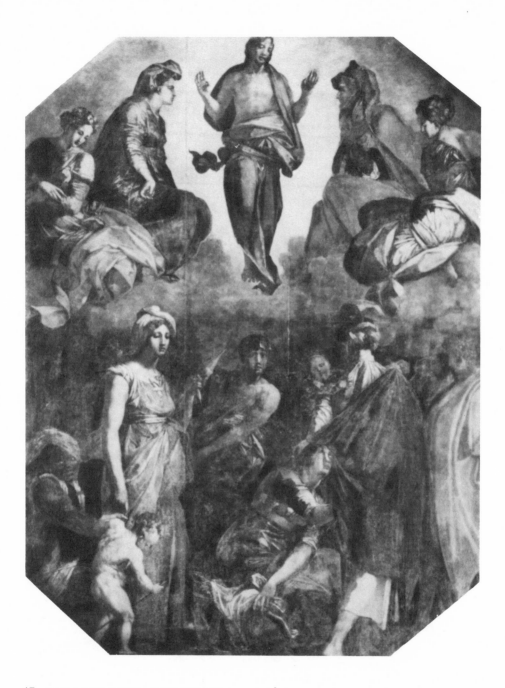

17   ROSSO FIORENTINO: TRANSFIGURATION. CITTÀ DI CASTELLO, CATHEDRAL

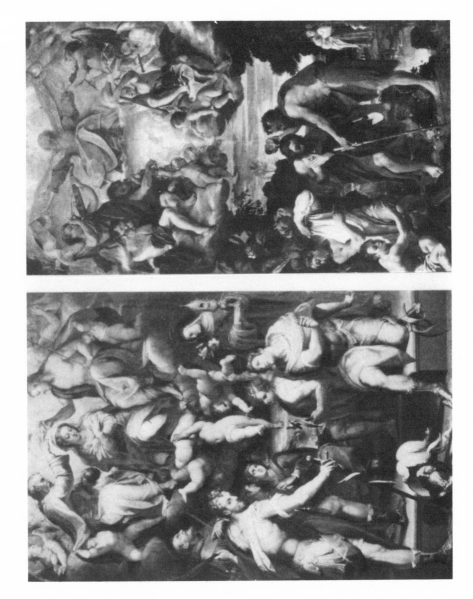

18 ORAZIO SAMACCHINI: CORONATION OF THE VIRGIN. BOLOGNA, PINACOTECA

19 ANNIBALE CARRACCI: BAPTISM OF CHRIST. BOLOGNA, S. GREGORIO

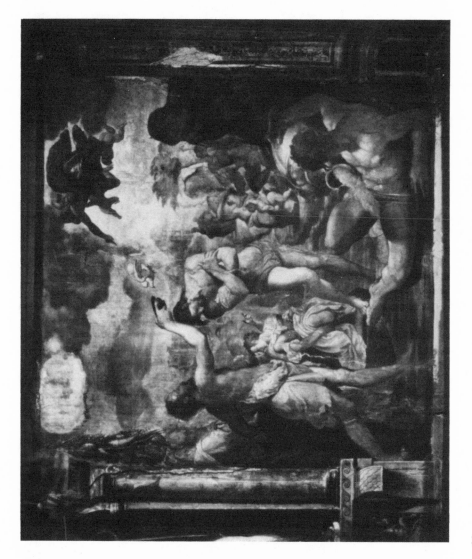

20 JACOPINO DEL CONTE: BAPTISM OF CHRIST. ROME, S. GIOVANNI DECOLLATO

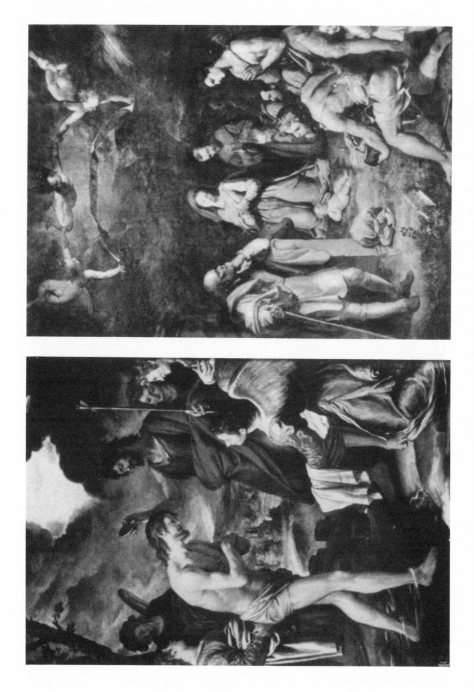

21 SANTI DI TITO: BAPTISM OF CHRIST. FLORENCE, GALLERIA CORSINI

22 SANTI DI TITO: NATIVITY. FLORENCE, S. GIUSEPPE

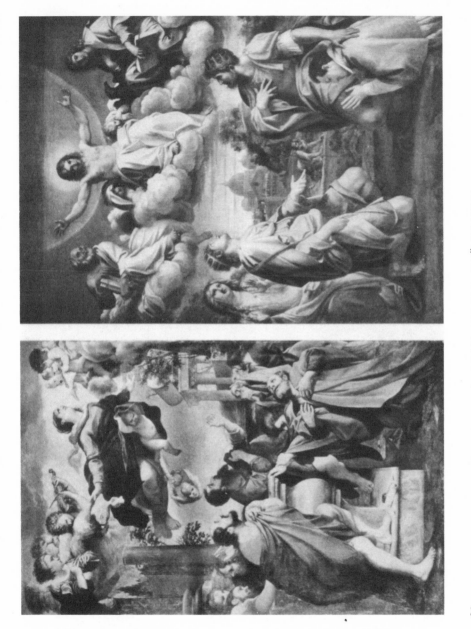

23 ANNIBALE CARRACCI: ASSUMPTION OF THE VIRGIN. DRESDEN, GEMÄLDEGALERIE

24 ANNIBALE CARRACCI: CHRIST IN GLORY. FLORENCE, PITTI

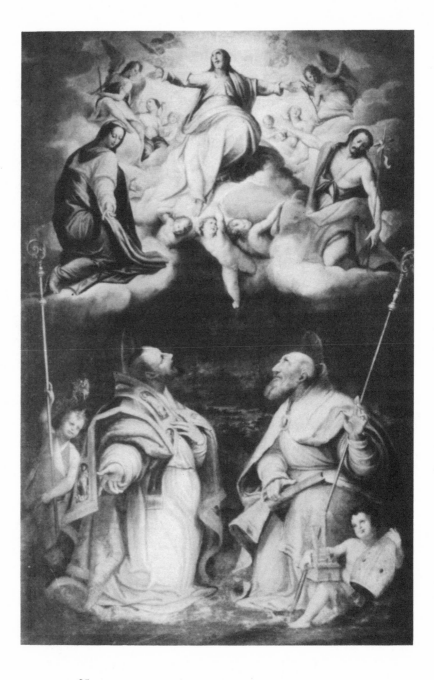

25 ORAZIO SAMACCHINI: CHRIST IN GLORY. BOLOGNA, S. PAOLO

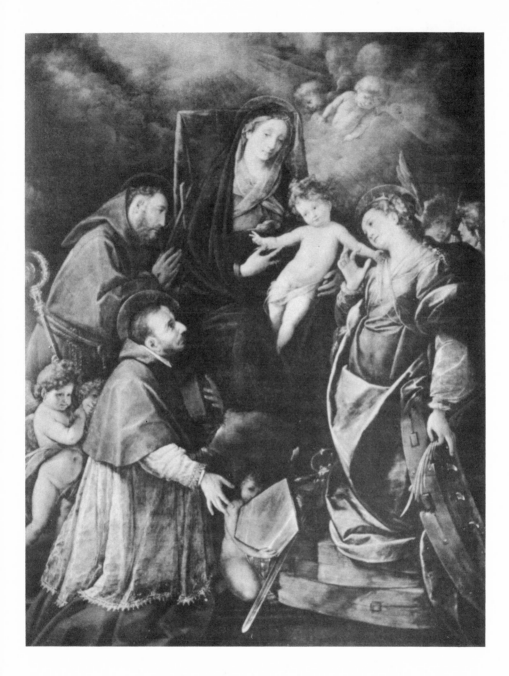

26 CERANO: MADONNA AND CHILD WITH SAINTS. FLORENCE, UFFIZI

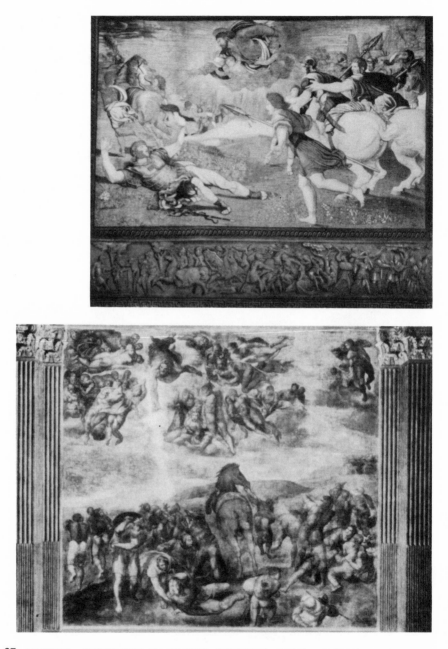

27 RAPHAEL: CONVERSION OF ST. PAUL (TAPESTRY). ROME, VATICAN

28 MICHELANGELO: CONVERSION OF ST. PAUL. ROME, VATICAN, CAPPELLA PAOLINA

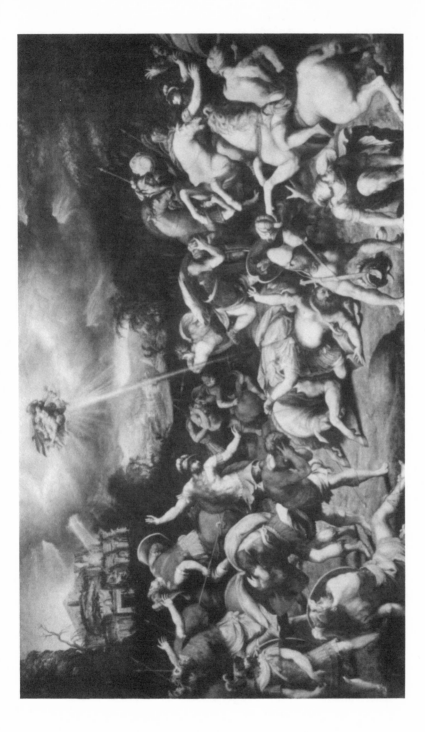

29 FRANCESCO SALVIATI: CONVERSION OF ST. PAUL. ROME, GALLERIA DORIA

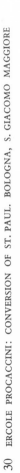

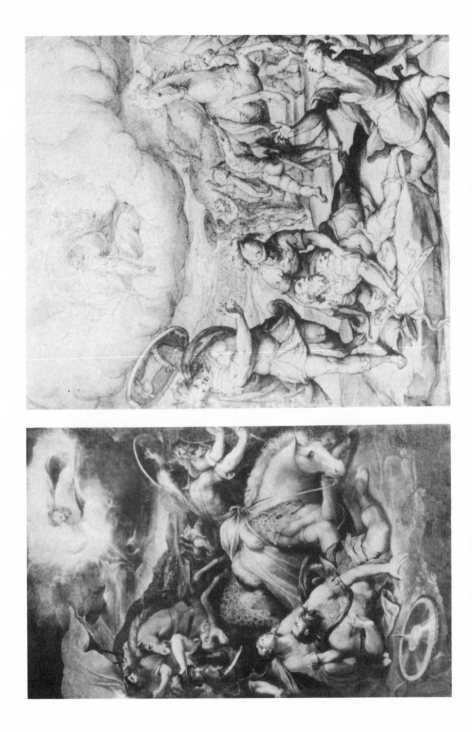

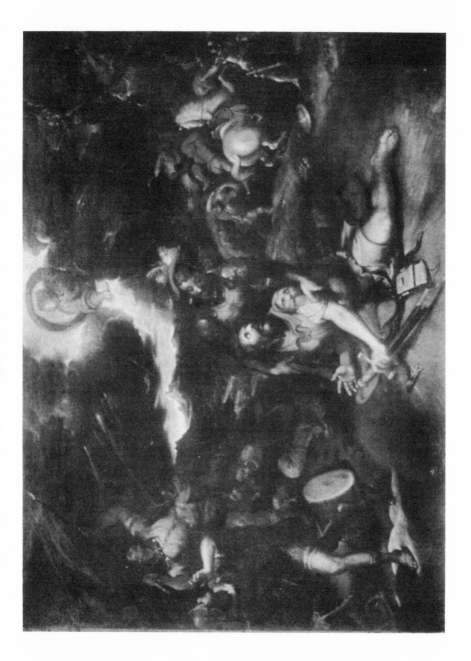

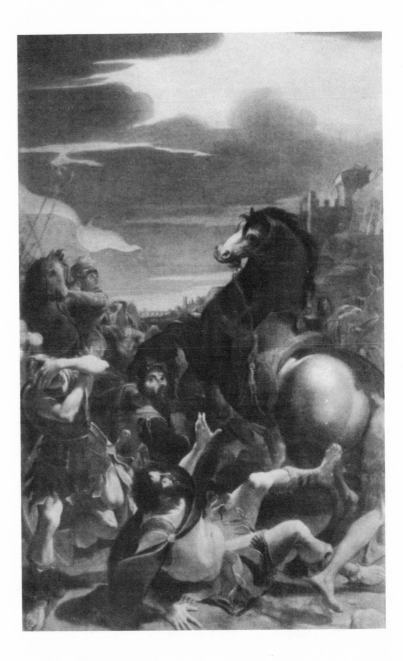

33 LODOVICO CARRACCI: CONVERSION OF ST. PAUL. BOLOGNA, PINACOTECA

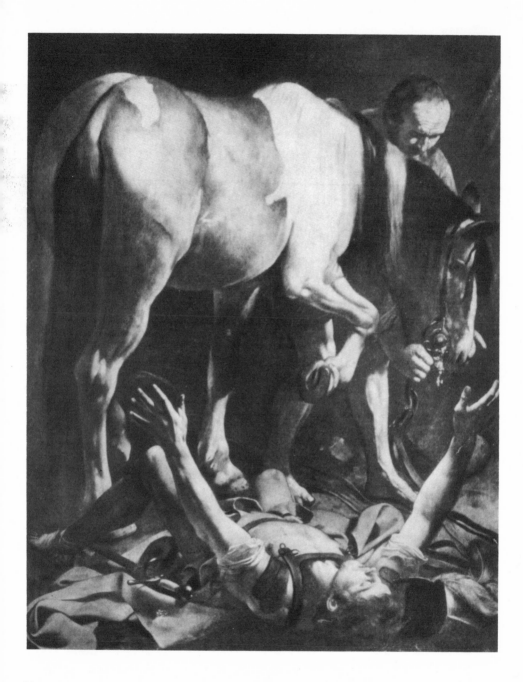

34 CARAVAGGIO: CONVERSION OF ST. PAUL. ROME, STA. MARIA DEL POPOLO

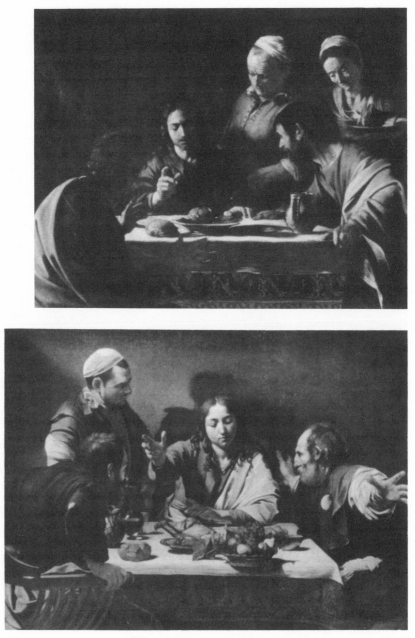

35   CARAVAGGIO: SUPPER AT EMMAUS. MILAN, BRERA

36   CARAVAGGIO: SUPPER AT EMMAUS. LONDON, NATIONAL GALLERY

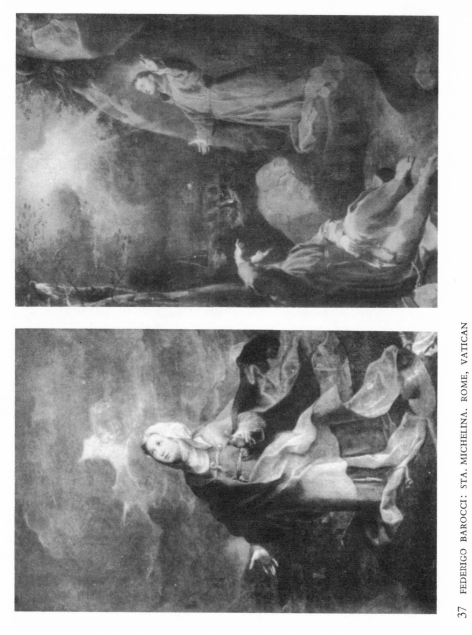

37 FEDERIGO BAROCCI: STA. MICHELINA. ROME, VATICAN

38 FEDERIGO BAROCCI: STIGMATIZATION OF ST. FRANCIS. URBINO, GALLERY

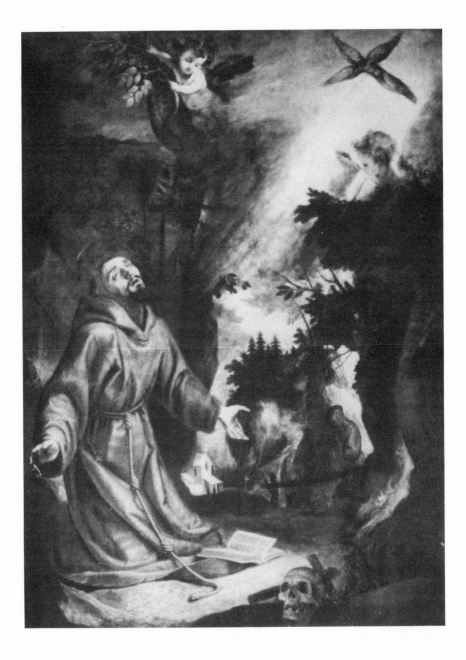

39　CIGOLI: STIGMATIZATION OF ST. FRANCIS. FLORENCE, MUSEO DI S. MARCO

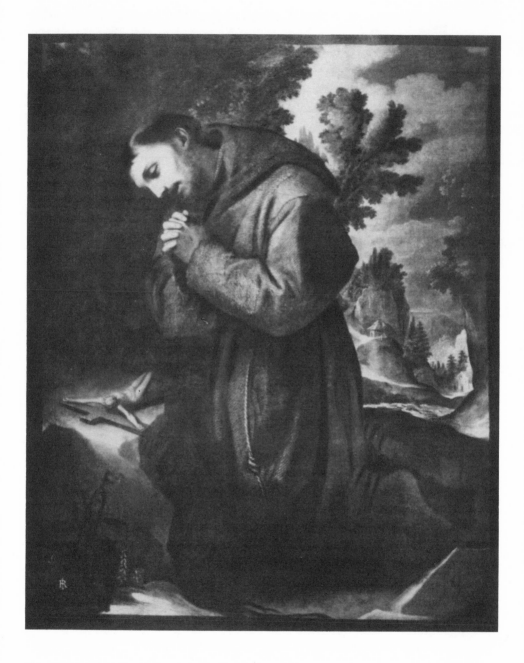

40   CIGOLI: ST. FRANCIS IN PRAYER. FLORENCE, PITTI

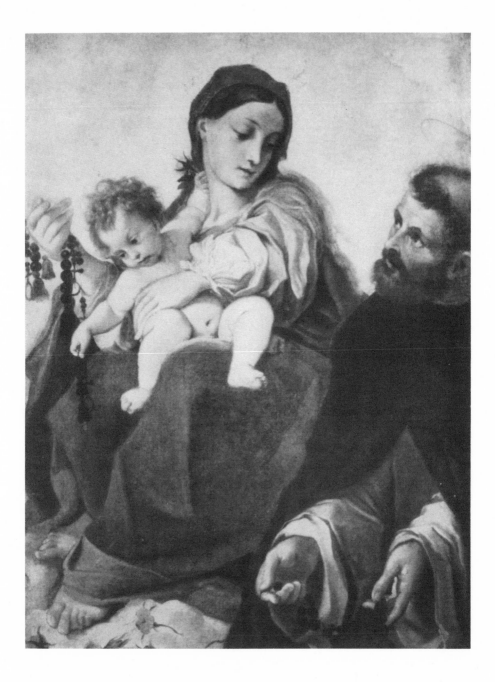

41   LODOVICO CARRACCI: MADONNA OF THE ROSARY. BOLOGNA, PINACOTECA

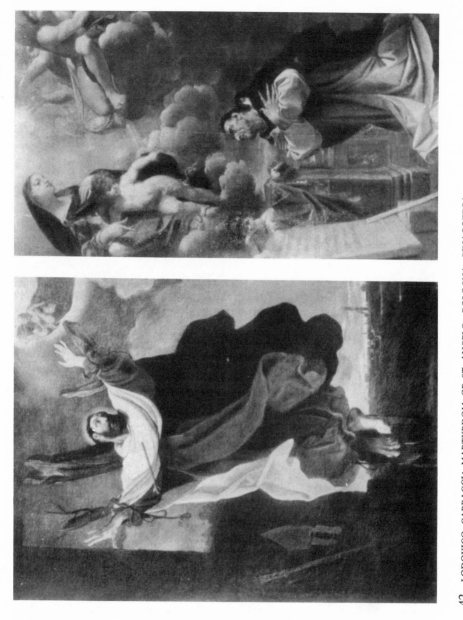

42 LODOVICO CARRACCI: MARTYRDOM OF ST. ANGELO. BOLOGNA, PINACOTECA

43 LODOVICO CARRACCI: MADONNA APPEARING TO ST. HYACINTH. PARIS, LOUVRE

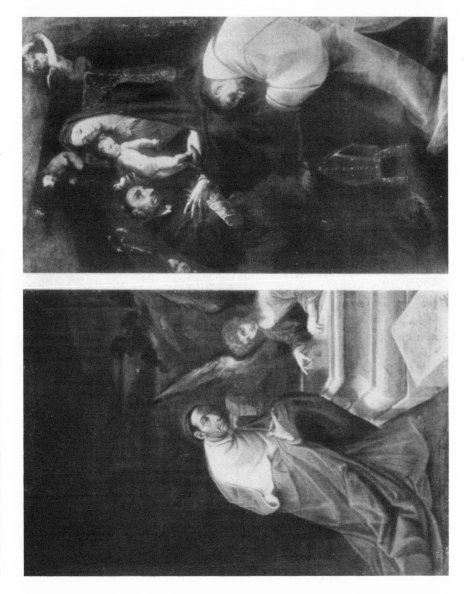

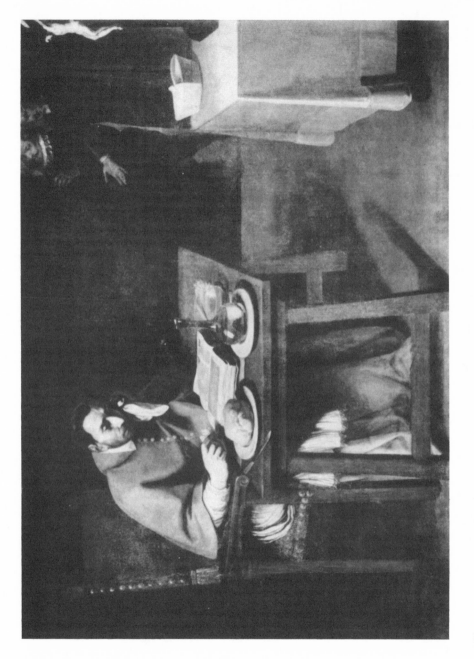

46 CRESPI: THE MEAL OF ST. CHARLES BORROMEO. MILAN, CHIESA DELLA PASSIONE

chiaroscuro niche, and go beyond Correggio in illusionism, as when a slip of drapery or a foot hangs over the frame into the world of the observer. This subjective optical quality is especially striking in the *St. George,* where the rearing body of the horse looms high in the foreground of the picture. Parmigianino again shows this preference for the illusionistic in his curious self-portrait in the convex mirror in Vienna, a trick (of exceedingly high quality to be sure) in which the hand, because it is so close to the mirror, appears unnaturally large. In this way, along with the optical painterly tendency, Parmigianino manifests his inclination toward the bizarre, the unnatural, the anticanonical.

In the course of his four years' stay in Rome (1523 to 1527), he established his personal style, developing it further to its finest maturity after the sack of Rome in 1527 caused him, as it did so many artists, to leave the Eternal City. Thus only a little later than Rosso and Pontormo, Parmigianino underwent the same transformation of style. In the harder Roman atmosphere the grace and softness of the Correggesque style is altered into a harder and stiffer structure, and from the delicate court ladies of Correggio develop heroines who, to be sure, are still graceful. This appears decisively in the one masterpiece of the Roman period which is preserved to us, the *Vision of St. Jerome* (Fig. 12), especially in its upper part, for the lower still shows a debt to Correggio.[21]

In contrast to the optical weaving of the figures, the *sfumato,* the lovely softness of the women of Correggio, Parmigianino's

[21] I think that here, in addition to connections with the *St. John* by Raphael in the Uffizi, one can also see others with Correggio's *Madonna with St. Sebastian* in Dresden. The Baptist takes the same central position as the St. Geminianus and looks outward with similar strain, and the spatial arrangement of the sleeping Jerome seen in foreshortening reflects the St. Roch in Correggio's painting. This last in any case must have been produced no earlier than around 1525, but Parmigianino could have seen studies of it, or drawings after it as well. To be sure, we would then have to place Parmigianino's painting around 1527 at the end of his Roman stay, following Vasari, and not at the beginning as Lili Fröhlich-Bum proposes in her book *Parmigianino* (Vienna, 1921), p. 22 (for which dating no impressive reasons are evident in any case).

composition is reduced to only a few figures with sharper contours, and the figure of the Madonna is of an outspoken monumentality. This is the attitude found in the later Raphael, in Sebastiano, in Michelangelo. But it is characteristic that the Michelangelo of the Sistine apparently exercised little influence on Parmigianino. The motif of the Madonna with the beautiful boy between her knees stems indeed from Michelangelo, but it goes back to a youthful work of the master, the *Madonna of Bruges*. Thus the placing of the Madonna is completely frontal. To this extent, and likewise in the type, the painting recalls "classic" feeling. What makes it more modern and anticlassic—in addition to its neglect of the spatial element—is its verticalism. Its frontality emphasizes its utterly unusual format, much more than twice as high as it is wide, a proportion we must recognize as offering an extreme contrast to Renaissance feeling, absolutely dedicated to balancing every relationship. Similarly the proportions of the Madonna are unusually elongated, and still more so in the sketch for the painting, now in the British Museum.[22] In the sketch the Madonna is presented standing on the clouds, the Child upright upon her left hip; the other hip is strongly curved and the figure is so elongated that it takes up three-fourths of the picture surface. Whence came this verticalism of Parmigianino's? He did not bring it with him from his home and the Correggio circle. Nor did he meet with it in the Rome of the 1520s—either within the Raphael school in Giulio Romano (even Peruzzi comes upon it only later in Siena) or among the Michelangelo followers such as Sebastiano. It was not until the end of the 1520s, and even then only in single instances, that Michelangelo's proportions began to stretch out lengthwise as if snapping apart. In any case he is in Florence, not in Rome. On the other hand, these changes of proportion, this verticalism, which are to be so characteristic of Mannerism in so many of its evocations, are already to be found at the beginning of the 1520s in that new anticlassical tendency of

[22] Compare the reproduction in Fröhlich-Bum, *Parmigianino*, p. 20.

Pontormo and Rosso. Besides, it develops that Rosso went to Rome in the same years as Parmigianino. For the history of early Mannerism it is certainly a significant fact that two leaders of the growing style, Rosso and Parmigianino, came together in Rome and worked beside each other during the years from 1523 to the terrible days of May, 1527. Even if little more can be established in detail, they can scarcely have failed to have been in contact.[23]

Thus, without venturing into the hypothetical, one can, on the basis of stylistic facts, deduce an exchange of influence. Rosso, who was in a position to look back on such brilliant and completely novel creations as the Volterra *Deposition* (even if he did not keep to the same level in Rome but fell into a strange hesitation) must have been the instigator, and must have made a significant impression on the much younger Parmigianino. He could tell him about the anticlassical artistic revolution in Florence, of which he was himself, along with Pontormo, one of the main participants. Compared to the heroic works of the High Renaissance, this style must have been a revelation to the sensitive young Parmigianino, whose whole temperament was desirous of novelty. And this explains the change in format, the new verticalism that is no mere external method, and the other similarities to the new style evident in Parmigianino's pictures.[24]

[23] The same engraver, Caraglio, who worked for Parmigianino, also worked for Rosso, whose very typical mannerist divinities in niches he, among others, engraved. Then too it is certainly no coincidence that Parmigianino's *St. Jerome* was commissioned for Città di Castello and that Rosso too soon thereafter (in 1528) delivered a strange Transfiguration for the cathedral of the same city. This at least permits the inference of the same circle of interested people and patrons.

[24] The heroine type of the Madonna which has been cited, in the *Vision of St. Jerome,* this noble figure with the rather strong features, the high-waisted costume which permits the broad, strong breast to come forward, may go back in general to the Roman attitude which tends to make things heroic and antique, and to be a development of the female type of the late Raphael and Michelangelo— the Sibyl by Peruzzi in Siena also shows a similar presentation in the costume and cut of the features. But Rosso's giant women, too, as already presented in his Florentine paintings such as the *Marriage of the Virgin,* may have played a part

Further, Parmigianino's conscious and entirely unclassical neglect of the canonical relation of figure to space may perhaps reflect the Florentine tendency, or at least be strengthened by it, even if he gives it other forms.

Both the excessive lengthening of the figure, and the neglectfulness in the handling of space, are acutely emphasized for the first time in a somewhat later painting, the famous, because especially charming, *Madonna of the Long Neck* (about 1535 to 1540, Fig. 13). Here the elongation of the body is the more thoroughgoing in that it does not involve the massive giantesses of Rosso, still partially visible in Parmigianino's own *Vision of St. Jerome,* but instead, a slim, elegant lady, an aristocrat, even more distinguished and courtly than Correggio's female saints. This uncanonical elongation enhances still further the elegance and the gracefully and carefully posed effect of the twisted position. The artistic method is the same, but the new proportions have a quite different meaning than in the ascetic Pontormo or in the excited Rosso. The angels have the same elegant grace, and the overlong nude leg of the youthful angel at the front, with the vase half cut off by the frame, carries a quite special accent.[25]

The spatial relations are astonishing. The group of the Virgin with the angels in front of the red curtain is set very high and off to one side; the eye must shift without transition into a deeper space where a column rises and a prophet, much too small in proportion to the group of the Virgin, stands holding a scroll. It is

in this. In the *Transfiguration* for Città di Castello, which still draws its impulse from his Florentine period, we find a female type very closely related to the *Vision* by Parmigianino.

[25] In Pontormo's masterpiece of the *Entombment* in Santa Felicità, the youthful angel which supports the body of Christ under its arm at the extreme side shows a certain parallel, even if not nearly so accentuated. The *Love Cutting his Bow* in Vienna, which belongs to the same period, also shows a certain relationship with the cowering angel in the foreground of Pontormo's painting. Parmigianino could have seen this painting shortly after it was produced, on his stopover in Florence in 1527 on his flight to Bologna. Yet Correggio's St. George in his Dresden *Madonna* may have served as a direct source for the angel with the vase, at least for the motif of the nude leg turned to the foreground.

the same evocation of intentionally unrealistic proportions in the sizes of the figures, in their relation to each other and in their positions in space, as in Pontormo's *Martyrdom of St. Maurice* (Pitti) of 1529 and as later in El Greco.[26]

Thus the Florentines did not (as has been suggested) take over Mannerism from Parmigianino; on the contrary, as is only natural considering his relative youth, he learned from the anticlassical movement of Pontormo and Rosso precisely those things that distinguish him from the preceding generation—the subjective rhythmic quality of his art, the uncanonical presentation of the figure, demonstrated in verticalism and in other elements, and the equally uncanonical handling of space. But Parmigianino is an independent artist. His color is quite different from that of the others; where Pontormo, originally following Andrea del Sarto, has soft flowing tones, less differentiated and though simplified greatly strengthened, and where Rosso forces local color and uses it dynamically to divide his layers and let them flicker in light, Parmigianino's coloring relies on the finest nuances. A kind of greenish general tone is spread over the whole, and to it are subordinated the local colors, running from moss green to pea green (in the *Madonna of the Long Neck*), with some reddish tones tossed in.[27] This and the flowing light (similar to Correggio) in themselves prove that Parmigianino does not create with plastic volumes like Rosso, nor of course so much from within outward

[26] The column was originally supposed to end in an architectural form (see the drawing illustrated by Fröhlich-Bum, *Parmigianino,* p. 44) but it was not executed, since the painting according to its inscription is "non finito." But a similar column also rises in the background in the ruined landscape of the *Holy Family* in the Uffizi, which was greatly influenced by Giulio Romano. Whether Parmigianino would really have carried the column higher seems questionable. The effect is too good as it is.

[27] In the Dresden painting with the Deacons, the hands of one and the same person are handled, in their painterly aspects, completely differently from each other: the hand on the red background is greenish and on the green background is reddish. This is not only a surprising optical observation of the effect of contrasting colors, but also a most unclassical trait. Correggio always treats the hands as equivalent and standardized.

as Pontormo. Despite the craftsmanlike contour element that with the subtlest sensitivity bounds his figures, the optical element always remains so essential that the linkage between the figures is set up less in a linear than in an optical way. Thus he never builds his figures exclusively by volume like Michelangelo and some of the mannerists; instead his figures always stand isolated and yet enclosed in space. Only this space is not proportionate to the figures in it, and it is here (as has been suggested), that he approaches tendencies of the early mannerist movement in Florence. He too uses, besides, the system of additive layers, and apparently takes this too from Florence; that is, he constructs three-dimensional space by parallel layers and thus brings it near the picture plane. This is already apparent in his early portraits (for instance, the very typical one of 1524 in Naples), but more insistently still in a late painting, the masterly Dresden picture of the Madonna with the Two Deacons seated before a balustrade. But he never interlaces or shuttles the layers, nor the figures either; the optical element of color and light plays such a part, that the effect is different, more loosely spatial, less stiff than in Tuscan Mannerism.[28] In the Dresden picture it is notable how far in space the Madonna in her glory of light on the clouds stands behind the balustrade figures. Individually Parmigianino's own is the "grazia" so famous in the Carracci circle. The infinite distinction of stance, the *recherché* and preciosity of movement and turn in the body, the transparency of narrow, exaggeratedly long-fingered hands expresses his artistic nature, albeit the predisposition was already provided in Correggesque art. This has nothing directly to do with Pontormo and Rosso, neither of them "elegant," but over and above Parmigianino, the individual, it expressed the new mannerist feeling.[29]

[28] Bedoli, who carries on Parmigianino's style in Parma, attaches himself much more closely to the Florentine procedure in space, in the additive layers, etc.

[29] Here too the extent to which the affectations of the *quattrocento* live on in Parmigianino would have to be investigated—so that one could establish a kind of archaism here too—and the extent to which mannerist and *quattrocento* "grace" differ from each other.

The grace of Parmigianino could the more easily influence Florentine Mannerism of the second generation, in that the ground was already laid in the work of Botticelli and others. Thus a mutual influence was possible, in that Parmigianino took over the bases of the new aspects of his style from the Florentine movement of 1520, but himself in turn—especially through his prints and drawings—had a reciprocal influence on Florence.

THE new style that cast off the classic, and against the Renaissance pattern of canonical balance, set up a subjective rhythmic figuration and an unreal space formation, rests essentially on these three personalities: Pontormo, Rosso, and Parmigianino. In Florence it developed out of the Andrea del Sarto circle as an outspoken reaction against the beauty and repose of the Florentine High Renaissance; between 1520 and 1523 it is already fully formed. In Rome, Parmigianino, himself an issue of Correggio's style, comes to Rosso's side. The sack of Rome in 1527 scattered the seeds of the new tendency far and wide, and it perhaps attained its wider significance in European history through that very fact. In Florence, Pontormo's work proceeds further, his masterpieces appear—the *Entombment*, the Louvre painting. Following a Michelangelesque period, which for a time brings him into direct dependence on that great man, he winds up with his strange frescoes for San Lorenzo, of whose monumental abstraction the only traces we have are in drawings. But in his pupil Bronzino his trend is carried on, not only in the portrait,[30] but above all in figure and space composition. From this point on is formed the "mannerist" trend so typical precisely of Florence. Rosso, after some wandering, comes to Fontainebleau and through his paintings and decorations in the new mannerist style (to which scrollwork also pertains) this "northern Rome" becomes the pilgrimage center for northern and especially Flemish artists.

[30] The contrast of mannerist portraits of Pontormo, Rosso, and Parmigianino with the Renaissance would require separate treatment.

Through Rosso and Primaticcio, his follower, the anticlassical style spreads through the northern countries. Parmigianino's works achieve a huge circulation in northern Italy; by way of Venice and the Bassano circle he (joined with Tintoretto, who also covers mannerist ground) becomes a decisive influence on the last and perhaps greatest practitioner of the mannerist style, El Greco. Over all lies the powerful shadow of Michelangelo. We have seen how anticlassical elements were present in him *a priori*. Yet Michelangelo, though he is so typically "anticlassic," is not of decisive influence on the actual establishment of the mannerist style around 1520. His influence begins in a direct way only with the Medici Chapel, and more significantly with the *Victor* in the field of sculpture, and in the field of painting with the *Last Judgment,* from which even a Tintoretto could not escape. The further development of the mannerist style cannot be followed here; our scope is limited to sketching its establishment in the twenties of the sixteenth century. It is not any too often possible to put one's finger so exactly on a turning point in the flow of artistic things, in the way in which the passage from Vasari—the voice of the public—in dealing with Pontormo's falling away from true art has enabled us to do. This also made it possible to point out the archaic elements so intrinsic to early Mannerism and, in Pontormo especially, to demonstrate the influence of the north.[31]

This turning point, then, is established for Pontormo by a document, but it applies not merely to this one artist personally; rather it is—to seize it stylistically by the hand—a general shift of style, in which Rosso and a little later Parmigianino participate, and which becomes the point of departure for a European movement.[32]

[31] In the portraits of Parmigianino too there has been thought to be visible something unItalian and subjectively northern (Fröhlich-Bum, *Parmigianino,* p. 32). In any case this element in Mannerism met the northern peoples halfway, which explains the remarkably quick picking-up of the same thing in the north.

[32] The particular position of Beccafumi ought to be considered for a more complete understanding. His relation to Sodoma is similar to Pontormo's and Rosso's relation to Andrea del Sarto, and Parmigianino's to Correggio, but be-

With Raphael's death classic art—the High Renaissance—subsided, though to be sure, like the "divine" Raphael himself it is immortal and will always come to life again in a new form. Its immediate successor is the new, anticlassical viewpoint—the mannerist-subjective, which now becomes dominant. Despite all the countercurrents this dominance persists for almost sixty years, until a new reaction is successful, a reaction deriving equally from the Carracci and the diametrically opposed Caravaggio, and consciously laying hold on the preceding period of the early *cinquecento*. Pontormo, Rosso, Parmigianino, with the genius of Michelangelo hovering above them and reaching beyond them, introduced this period, which is not a mere transition, not merely a conjunction between Renaissance and Baroque, but an independent age of style, autonomous and most meaningful.[33]

ing in Siena he does not have the European influence as they do, and is thus not of such direct significance for the rise of the style.

[33] The question arises: is there any broad explanation in the history of culture for this apparently sudden change of style? For the appearance of weariness, of reaction against the all too great beauty and stability of high classic art, could scarcely cover the matter and satisfy as a single explanation. Doubtless reasons may be found in the general viewpoint of the period. Certainly parallel indications can be found in literature and in music; yet to establish any such interchange of influence among the arts one would have to have a mastery of the materials reaching into detail if one would avoid arriving at mere generalizations. The materials of religious ferment are certainly present in the time in all sufficiency, and they perhaps explain also the turn toward the spiritual which characterizes the beginning of the movement. But it would be difficult to find causes for this (parallels are something else). There is interest in the extraordinarily free observation by Giordano Bruno, cited by Julius Schlosser in *Die Kunstliteratur des Manierismus* (Vol. VI of *Materialien zur Quellenkunde der Kunstgeschichte*), p. 110, "The artist alone is the creator of the rules and rules exist just so far and are just so many as there are artists." Yet this is only stated for the art of poetry. In the field of the theory of art compare, besides, the quotations cited in Schlosser's materials, Panofsky, *Idea*, 1924 (p. 39 ff., "Mannerism.") I have devoted a thorough review to this important book elsewhere.

THE ANTI-MANNERIST STYLE

SOMETIME around 1590, in any event toward the end of the sixteenth century, there occurred a palpable break in the stylistic development of Italian painting. It marks the conclusion of a sixty- to seventy-year period which, though lacking absolute homogeneity, possessed a strongly defined character, especially in the Tuscan mainstream of artistic tradition. In the course of time this character underwent certain transformations which, almost more than the original style itself, were clearly diagnosed as symptoms of disease by the theorists of the seventeenth century. They were so regarded also by a group of men who actively opposed the dominant tendency and who finally conquered it. A kind of reaction took place, based on a certain bourgeois regulatory consciousness, an almost automatic attack upon an artistic concept which, through exaggerations of its original nature, and even more through endless repetitions, betrayed unmistakable signs of overbreeding, and hence of sterility. This was generally the case with the style which had been dominant in Italy since about 1520 and which today is commonly known as "manneristic."

What does *maniera* mean? Literally: "making by hand"; a manual activity or skill. *Maniera* gradually came to be synonymous with "mode" in the sense of "style" or "manner"—Vasari's "maniera bizantina cioè greca." But the concept of mere manual activity, of handiwork, still remained. Vasari says about sculptors (*Scultura,* Chapter I), "They usually make the hair on the head of a statue thick and curly, *più di maniera che di natura.*" This means that in such passages the hand works almost mechanically; the sculptor needs no model from nature, but follows a specific prototype, or the established precepts of a school. This mechanical attitude engenders conformity or, in other words, "manner." Accordingly a manner is something unoriginal, since it always repeats manually something predetermined—often so exactly that it becomes tedious and unbearable. Today we would use the expression "cliché" or "carbon copy." When this empty stereotyping utilizes forms or formulae inherited from a style already abstract, anormative, and remote from nature, the result must necessarily be something merely decorative or ornamental. This is what generally happened to pictorial practice, especially in Florence and Rome, but also in Bologna, Parma, and so on in the second half of the sixteenth century. Only this style—and we must call it a style because of its wide diffusion—is actually "di maniera," or "mannered." It utilized the relatively abstract forms which had been created and erected into a system by the revolutionaries against the High Renaissance—Pontormo, Rosso, Parmigianino, and even Bronzino. Out of these it manufactures objects for all kinds of religious and secular purposes—church pictures as well as palace decorations. In much the same way Expressionism today has been turned to account in stage settings and the decor of art students' balls.

Thus it was that the older style (which I have called "anti-classical," for lack of a better word, but which is usually termed "manneristic" by a process of reverse derivation from its offshoot) became "mannered." In other words, the noble, pure, idealistic, and abstract style, lasting approximately from 1520 to 1550, was transformed in the succeeding phase (about 1550 to 1580) into a manner; it became "di maniera" by repetition, cleverness, and playful exaggeration on the one hand, by weak concessions on the other. The "healthy" will of certain discerning people was directed only against this then-present danger. They felt that an extraordinary decline in quality had taken place since the High Renaissance, which was already accepted as "classic"; and in their eyes the only cure for art lay in a return to the tested principles of that period, whether in Rome, in Parma, or in Venice. Hence the purification, the reform, the "restaurazione della pittura" which was attempted and accomplished, and which was referred to as such in seventeenth-century writings on art (Bellori, Malvasia), was not directed against the works of the early and mature periods of Mannerism: that is to say, not against Pontormo, Parmigianino, or Rosso, whose works were not much considered at this period anyway.[1] The real damage, the pressing danger, was felt to come from their own contemporaries, or from the men of a slightly older generation who had brought about the "decline" (if one may still be permitted the use of that word over the veto of the Vienna school) of this artistic tradition.[2] Logically, of course, the original anticlassical Mannerism would be included in this healing process, for its principles formed the basis for the late phase which was to be combated. The attack was directed not only against

[1] Cigoli, however, in his early period still copied Pontormo. It is striking that Filippo Baldinucci in his *Notizie de' Professori del disegno da Cimabue in qua* . . . does not take up Pontormo, Rosso, and Bronzino; he treats their immediate predecessor Andrea del Sarto and then jumps to Stradano and late Mannerism.

[2] Carlo Cesare Malvasia in *Felsina Pittrice* (Bologna, 1673), I, 358, enumerates (though rather at random) some of these *maniera* artists: "Furono questi il Salviati, i Zuccheri, il Vasari, Andrea Vicentino, Tomaso Laureti. . . ." and from Bologna: "il Samacchino, il Sabbatino, il Calvarte, i Procaccini e simili, che . . . totalmente nella loro immaginativa si fondarono, e ad un certo fare sbrigativo, e *affatto manieroso* s'applicarono." Compare also the important passage in Giovanni Pietro Bellori, *Vite de' Pittori* (Rome, 1672), p. 20: "e gli Artefici abbandonando lo studio della natura, vitiarono l'arte con la *maniera,* o vogliamo dire fantastica idea. . . . Questo vitio distruttore della pittura cominciò da prima a germogliare in maestri di honorato grido, e si *radicò nelle scuole,* da che seguirono poi: onde non è credibile a raccontare quanto degenerassero non solo da Rafaelle, ma da gli altri, che *alla maniera diedoro cominciamento."* (Italics added.)

mannerist form, although this was the center of the argument; the spirit which underlay this by now completely unfruitful artistic trend had also to be thoroughly altered. *Di maniera—di natura.* Hence an instinctive opposition was directed against the ecstatic quality so clearly displayed at the beginning of the manneristic movement against the spiritualism which sought a deepening of content through primitivism and spatial and corporeal abstraction. It was not a literary or a theoretical opposition, but was carried on simply by means of objectivity and practical work, which best demonstrates the transformation of artistic feeling. But the real enemy was, as we have said, the mannered Mannerism of the second phase, against whose shallowness, even in spiritual matters, the reform which set in around 1580 was directed. The aggressive purpose of the new movement was to cut loose from the degeneration of form just as much as from the degeneration of the spiritual into the playful and allegorical. A healthy down-to-earth spirit came into existence, paralleling a vigorous treatment of form achieved through purposeful work and a renewed contact with living reality. If a certain prosiness was to be the price of rationality, it was not shunned. It is thus understandable that an outspokenly realistic tendency could now for the first time appear openly.

Basically the reformers had no very difficult task. They were tearing down a building which was already crumbling. As is almost always the case in such periods, there were very many and very industrious artists who puttered along at Mannerism displaying slight stylistic variations; among them were talented men, capable and witty as well as entertaining decorators and designers of ornament, but there was not one outstanding personality in the whole lot. The only man in this period who was really different, who bore within himself real seeds of future development, Federigo Barocci, lived apart and did not belong to the same line of development as the *maniera* people. Venetian art had a similar life apart (even if not quite so isolated as was formerly thought), a life which, in the critical period of which we are speaking, was nearing its end. But in Florence and Rome artists of the third and fourth rank set the pace, names which in a naïve art history (if I may use the expression) did not endure at all. To this group belong all these artists "de petite manière" who worked in the *Studiolo* of Francesco I: Macchietti, Naldini, Poppi, Stradano, and so on. It is only in our own day of zealous art historians that a fluttering of life has been breathed into them again. It also includes the painters of large scale frescoes; Vasari and Salviati (who reveals a somewhat stronger character); Alessandro Allori who flooded all Tuscany with his insipid pictures; and correspondingly in Rome, the even less enjoyable and more pretentious apparition of Federigo Zuccaro, Barocci's cousin. Santi di Tito (so wittily lampooned by Tintoretto), although more reactionary and more conservative, also belongs in this series to some extent. In opposition to these handy-men of the *maniera* arose artists who, although not all of the same age, were all born in the last third of the century, in different places. Very different as to temperament and character, and sharply contrasting in their artistic activities though they were, they shared certain traits in common— the desire for simplicity and objectivity instead of complexity, for truth to nature (or that part of nature that could be objectively tested) instead of to the "imaginative," and for solid and dedicated work instead of painting by rote with only a glib and facile "effect" in mind. To name only the most important, the group included the Carracci in Bologna, Cigoli in Florence, and (a number of years younger) Caravaggio, the Lombard, in Rome, and Cerano in Milan. Their conception of art, their position toward religion and the transcendental, is to be the subject of this study.

It must be remembered that such crises, such shifts and transformations, necessarily take place with some overlapping. While some of the reformers are just beginning their work, the older generation is still working. The taste of the public and of the patron does not change so quickly, and a superimposition of various layers of taste takes place (even without considering the relation to other countries, into which Mannerism came as an imported commodity). Thus some of the *maniera* group could still be active and accepted far beyond the turn of the century [3] even though forced to make occasional concessions to the new, more realistic, trend of taste. On the other hand the reformers themselves were not completely sure of their direction, and would still waver back and forth, even in their spiritual conceptions, between the accustomed superficiality and the seriousness of the new forms. For after all, they had all studied under the masters of the past generation, and been brought up on their works—under Alessandro Allori and Santi di Tito; Tibaldi and Samacchini; Fontana and Campi, and so on. It took a great deal of work and will power to imbue the inherited forms with the new spirit, or to discard them entirely.

And now the question arises, what did they put in their place? Where did they look for nature as opposed to *maniera?* Along what path did they seek a cure? First of all through knowledge— learning to draw, copying pictures, studying anatomy—in short through the usual fundamentals as they can be learned in academies. The significant position of the academies, their emphasis on the teachability and learnability of art, were certainly among the signs of the times, but their influence was perhaps not quite so important as is often represented. Academies or similar institutions were nothing particularly new at the time. The *maniera*

[3] This is true of El Greco, in whom the flame of original, true, and spiritual Mannerism again bursts into life with completely unprecendented vehemence. But it should not be forgotten that this could happen only in the special circumstances of Toledo, that is, far from the specifically "modern" art movement of central Italy. It is idle to wonder how El Greco would have developed if he stayed longer in Rome on his trip at the end of the seventies, or if he had stayed permanently. We can get a little light on the subject from the odd genre composition of his early years: the youth, accompanied by a peasant and an ape, blowing on a glowing charcoal—a Bassanesque and also a pre-Caravaggesque motif. The flamboyant forms of his later period can hardly be imagined in the Rome of the nineties.

generation was heavily afflicted with industriousness and zeal for learning. Indeed it would be hard to find a more industrious or more culture-mad man than Federigo Zuccaro. He was the typical "princeps academiae" just as Vasari was a thoroughgoing academician. One even gains the impression that the high cultural level of the artist may have sunk a little in the new generation, and that this may also have been part of the "cure." Of the three Carracci, only Agostino (the least significant) is the cultivated one, but he was not therefore more highly regarded by his older cousin Lodovico, and he was positively ridiculed by his brother Annibale for his learned prating and his discourses on art. Cigoli, of course, still belonged to the generation of cultivated painters, and was also an architect and a poet. About Cerano we know little, save for his love of hunting (not very intellectual); and Caravaggio was definitely anarchistic, bohemian, and decidedly anticultural.

What is absent from the thought of all these men is the theoretical side. They did not theorize nearly so much as the *maniera* people who, insofar as they were not merely superior house painters, arranged and delivered lectures, wrote treatises, concocted theories of art, and were, in general, literary minded. All of this was done away with as far as possible in the healing process. After Lomazzo and Zuccaro (who belonged to an older generation), scribbling on the theory of art stopped for a while, and so did the academy lectures, which Zuccaro had founded. Only with the increasing classicism of the second half of the seventeenth century does art theory begin to come alive again, based this time on a firmer foundation. The generation of which we are now speaking had too much to do in the way of practical accomplishments to permit itself the luxury of theorizing. Its strength was not created from this, and just as little from increased academic activity, except insofar as the academy encouraged the grasping of reality and the training of the eye on the model.

These artists of the new generation sought the basis for the "cure" in the conception of form either antedating the so-called anticlassic Mannerism or not touched by it. By and large, what I call the "grandfather law" is at work here—that is, a generation, with deliberate disregard for the views and feelings of the generation of its fathers and direct teachers, skips back to the preceding period and takes up the very tendencies against which its fathers had so zealously struggled, albeit in a new sense. Therefore it corresponds to the subjectivistic revolution of 1520 against the too-beautiful and too-balanced qualities of the High Renaissance, against its normatives, and its taken-for-granted rationale. This art reached back toward older archaistic tendencies (to which the acceptance of Nordic elements also belongs). By the same process the conservative reaction that took place throughout Italy in the eighties and nineties went back to the solid foundation of Renaissance painting as a cure for the Mannerism of the generation of its fathers, and built upon that. The question now arises as to how the transcendental element comes into its own, and what fate befalls it under such an unspeculative and objective attitude, which expresses itself in the gradations varying from moderate idealism to what is, at least for that period, a crass naturalism. For the church—and we are still in the midst of the period of the Counter Reformation—made no fewer demands on art in the representation of sacred subjects than it had in the preceding period. How will such an artistic phase, seeking and needing reform, look upon the ecstatic, the visionary? Will the heavens still open? Will the human be deified, apotheosized? Or will the divine be humanized?

In this new pictorial conception, opposed to the manneristic and the mannered, what first strikes the eye, even in religious pictures, is the formal transformation of pictorial structure. The new conquest of space and the natural assimilation of figures into space, in sharp contrast to the ornamental, theoretical jumbling of volumes in Mannerism, are striking and pervasive factors of the new style. The new density and weight of the pigment stands out against the pale, abstract wash techniques of the earlier style. Thus, corporeal and material elements are by now strongly emphasized, and give the whole aspect of the new picture something natural, something earthbound, something thoroughly understandable. Hand in hand with this transformation of the formal concept toward greater simplicity and naturalness (which must self-evidently be based on a general spiritual revolution) the spirit and meaning of the thematic content also changes. A specifically iconographic change is often not demonstrable, since in many cases a precise ecclesiastical form had been fixed once and for all. Hence one cannot avoid a formal analysis, since only thus can the new meaning of the iconographically unchanged picture be revealed. But, beyond this, as we shall see, the forthright, unspeculative thought of the new style often alters the thematic material, sometimes to a surprising degree.

Let us now test a few examples of antimanneristic treatment of transcendental themes by the individual artists whom we have characterized as the principal reformers. We shall first select a work—as characteristic and uncomplicated as possible—by the oldest of this group, Lodovico Carracci, a man much underrated today as regards both his artistic quality and his art historical importance. The so-called *Madonna degli Scalzi* (Fig. 14) shows the Madonna standing on the crescent moon—a motif that certainly comes from the North, where it is especially common in German sculpture. Appearing also in Italy in the sixteenth century, it comes into general use in the seventeenth century among the Bolognese, and after that, above all, in Spain. The Child bends down from His mother's arms toward the rapt figure of St. Francis, and lays his little hand in the deeply tanned hand of the saint. On the other side kneels St. Jerome, looking upward at the Madonna, and angels making music seem to disappear into the broad aureole of light drawn around the head of the Purissima. It is thus a conception of the utmost simplicity. One would look in vain through all pre-Carraccesque art for a representation so simple and yet so imbued with noble and elevated feeling. How far superior it is to everything that Prospero Fontana, Lodovico's teacher, was able to paint in his provincial way. For Bolognese painting before the Carracci—from Bagnacavallo to Samacchini, Sabbatini, Tibaldi, and so on—is, with few exceptions, of a wavering and *retardataire* character. But even when one turns to Florence, the focal point of Mannerism in the sixteenth century, how energetic is the break that Lodovico (who knew Florence well) made with the *maniera* generation. Let us compare, just to adduce a gross contrast, the well-known picture of the *Immaculate Conception* by Vasari, which he himself describes exhaustively in his autobiography (painted for Santi Apostoli at the beginning of the forties, and a later version in Lucca, which I show here, Fig. 15). The Virgin on the crescent moon, surrounded by angels, sets her foot on the head of the tempter, the serpent, whose body twines about the tree. To its withered branches are bound Adam and Eve, Moses and Aaron, David, and the other patriarchs and prophets, as we know them from representations of Limbo. This famous image, to which later artists like Chimenti d'Empoli are still bound, is quite typical for the symbolic outlook of the sixteenth century. The representation of the mystery of the Immaculate Conception, which in those days was so strongly in the foreground of ecclesiastical debates (although it was not raised to a dogma until the nineteenth century), was especially suited to this kind of literary and exegetical attempt.[4] Vasari's picture is in every respect contrary to the new spirit which Lodovico represents—formally by the filling of the space with bodies, by the decorative and ornamental elements (e.g., the crossed bodies of Adam and Eve in the foreground), by the pseudo-Michelangelesque poses, by the use of graphic detail in place of color. Even more striking is the difference in spiritual content, with the petrification of all emo-

---

[4] On the different representations of the *conceptio immaculata* see K. Künstle, *Ikonographie der christlichen Kunst* (Freiburg im Breisgau, 1928), I, 646, and the references quoted there (particularly Graus, 1905).

tional content into allegorical abstraction. But Lodovico is certainly not representing a specific *conceptio immaculata* in his *Madonna degli Scalzi*. The Christ Child in the Virgin's arms, and also the presence of the two saints are not customary in a *conceptio immaculata* by strict definition—indeed they are rather unthinkable. To us it is all the more significant, therefore, that in spite of such inconsistencies, this vision of the Virgin standing on the new moon, has become for multitudes *the* image of the Immaculata.[5] For indeed this beautiful and famous work of Lodovico's was one of the main instigators of the seventeenth-century representation of the Immaculata stripped of allegorical and symbolic trimmings —the Madonna set off against a light-colored nimbus and clouds floats on the crescent moon, supported or surrounded by angels; she soars in the air, exalted and often in rapturous ecstasy. Following Lodovico's pattern closely, his pupil Guido Reni represents the Virgin on the crescent moon (this time specifically as the Immaculata) with the nimbus of rays framed by a garland of angels covering almost the whole upper portion of the picture (Forli). His direct influence is perhaps responsible for those countless images of the Immaculata in Spain—some of them very famous—of which Murillo's are the most universally popular.[6] The allegorical

[5] Compare, among others, Alfred Woltmann and Karl Woermann, *Geschichte der Malerei* (Leipzig, 1879, ff.), III, 126; A. Riegl, *Entstehung der Barockkunst* (Vienna, 1908), p. 168; Künstle, *Ikonographie* I, 656, also places Lodovico's picture among the representations of the Immaculate Conception. One feature that leads to this conclusion is the crescent moon, which is often encountered in these representations, and another is the presence of St. Francis. For it was the Franciscans who, for their Officium (which was approved by Sixtus IV around 1480), first adopted the prayer of the "Immaculate Conception."

[6] Guido Reni received the commission for a similar picture, "una beata Vergine in mezze a duoi angeli, reppresentante la Immacolata Concezione" from the Infanta of Spain. After all kinds of misadventures, which are related by Malvasia, *Felsina Pittrice,* II, 37, the picture came into the hands of the Spanish ambassador to Rome, and hence it apparently exercised a direct influence upon Spanish painting. Yet the picture of the Immaculata in the Academia di San Fernando in Madrid must also be considered; it is correctly ascribed to the Cavalier d'Arpino by H. Voss, *Die Malerei der Spätrenaissance* (Berlin, 1920), p. 588 f. It is not yet

representation of the Conception, with its reference to the miraculous conquest of Original Sin, is withdrawn in favor of the pure figure of the *immaculata concepta* herself, the Purissima.

The warm and human realization of even the visionary and the transcendental, therefore, is what distinguishes this figure by Lodovico from the abstraction and rationalism of the mannerist conception, and enables it to become the prototype of a new conception which became dominant in the seventeenth century. It is a part of this same general change in outlook which reduces all the symbolic and abstruse trappings to one single intuitively comprehensible token, the crescent moon. This new feeling is also expressed in the optical illusion of proximity to the subject and in the fullness of the color range,[7] which is oriented again toward the great age of Venetian painting with its chromatic richness.

The acceptance of Correggio, documented both by the handling of light (as in the imposing head of aged St. Jerome) and in the optical foreshortening of the Christ Child, is also important for future developments. Nevertheless the work as a whole is not eclectic, at least no more so than that of the earlier Bolognese; on the contrary it has a truly individual note, attuned to a very special kind of lyricism. Lyricism itself is something foreign to the allegorical and theorizing vein of the *maniera,* and is especially unsuited to the linear and schematic elements of that style. The appearance of landscape (which neither could nor did play any role in the extreme Mannerism of Tuscany) at this time, toward the end of the century, and precisely in the circle of the Carracci, is a clear sign. For landscape usually contains a strong lyrical element. We are here dealing, therefore, with the intrusion of a subjective realm, expressed and emphasized through the optical aids of color and light. It exists through realization rather than construction.

---

clear what the relation in time between this picture and Reni's may be. But the fact that it represents a crowning of Mary puts it in another type.

[7] Lodovico was one of the first to paint on a ground of red-brown bolus, and this gives his pictures a certain heaviness which is different from the manneristic technique.

We shall arrive at the same conclusions if we consider another work, wholly different from the first in its general disposition, again chosen from the extensive, though uneven, works of Lodovico. It too is a visionary representation—the *Transfiguration* (Bologna, Pinacoteca, Fig. 16).[8] In this work, designed for the high altar of San Pietro, lyrical idealism was not so important as dynamic impact, which had to be strong enough to be perceptible at a distance. Nevertheless the relation of this to a mannerist picture is essentially the same as in the previous example, both in form and spirit. It stands in the same relation to Rosso's *Transfiguration* in Città di Castello (Fig. 17) as does Lodovico's *Madonna degli Scalzi* to Vasari's *Conception*. In Rosso's painting, too (really a paraphrase of the *Transfiguration*), the intellectual, the symbolic, and the odd predominate, although it dates from the beginning of the mannerist movement (before 1530)—indeed to such a degree that even Vasari found it noteworthy ("e quivi fece mori, zingani, e le più strane cose del mondo") and wondered whether Rosso's painting had really been conceived according to the patron's intentions. Lodovico on the other hand went back to the simple, generally understandable representation of the Transfiguration which nonetheless revealed the mystery. Above soars Christ in "garments white and shining" between Moses and Elijah, below are the three awe-struck apostles, just as Raphael had painted the scene in the upper half of his famous work. A more immediate influence, perhaps, was exerted on Lodovico by Titian's late *Transfiguration* in San Salvatore, with the large, colorful, hazy Apostle figures in the foreground. The influence of Correggio, especially of his wildly agitated male figures from San Giovanni, can be very clearly traced. The result is a work which breaks completely with everything manneristic. Based on a strong movement of light and of compact masses, its bodies surge into the space, filling it both actually and optically. The work of Lodovico strikes us as more

[8] See my article "Contributo alla cronologia e all'iconografia di Lodovico Carracci" in *Cronache d'Arte*, III (1926), pp. 1–15, for the establishment of the date of the painting, which must be placed around 1595.

purely "baroque" than that of any of his fellow reformers—much more so than that of his cousins Annibale and Agostino. It is characterized by the dynamic release of voluminous forms, in relation to which light plays a special kind of role. The change from his Bolognese predecessors is immediately visible. Since we have lost track of the various Transfigurations by Bagnacavallo, Tibaldi, Camillo, and Giulio Cesare Procaccini mentioned in Malvasia, we must turn for purposes of comparison to some equally famous composition on as grand a scale, for instance Orazio Samacchini's *Coronation of the Virgin* (Bologna, Pinacoteca, Fig. 18).

Although the Carracci, including Lodovico, did not disdain this performance of their predecessor, as their adoption of many of its features reveals, nonetheless the difference is infinitely greater than any individual resemblance. Everything is *maniera*—the crowding of the figures, the tormented and twisted poses, and the cold colors with their iridescent hues. In Lodovico, by contrast, the decorative stiffness is dissolved, and the few figures are imbued with a new spirit, pulsating with life. The same holds true if one looks for a comparison outside Bologna. The *Resurrection* of the late mannerist Federigo Zuccaro, for all its jerky excitement, remains purely ornamental. Lodovico, in contrast to all of these, leads the way to a new development both in form and spirit; his influence is far greater than one might suppose from reading the latest surveys of the period, in which Lodovico is dismissed with a couple of words.

The *Communion of St. Jerome* by Agostino Carracci, older than his brother Annibale, is certainly an outstanding example of the new feeling for form and matter. But this important painting has as little to do with the new treatment of the transcendental as the rest of Agostino's painstaking but rather dry compositions. (Some, such as his *Assumption,* are more or less irrelevant.)

On the other hand the art of the younger brother, Annibale, is of pervasive importance for the transformation of transcendental themes in the new restrained and self-controlled spirit. In comparison with Lodovico, one is struck in Annibale's work by the greater compactness of the parts, by the powerful yet more refined handling of the chiaroscuro, and by the normative (later on even definitely classical) depiction of corporeal volume and physical setting. Relations to Correggio are undeniable, especially in the early years, but not as great as has been supposed. The coloristic fusion of Correggio, the elegance of Parmigianino, have given way in Annibale's work to a much heavier conception, and his tonal harmonies are extraordinarily warm and full. Tendencies in the new direction appear even in the very early pictures with their sweet color. In the *Baptism of Christ* in San Gregorio of 1585 (Fig. 19) the picture plane is still cluttered with figures. They are stuck uncomfortably into each other. The boy in the foreground has much that is manneristic in his pose (by way of Parmigianino, perhaps also Tintoretto); the elaborate vision of the opening sky with its heavenly hosts is strongly influenced by Parma. It is a typically youthful picture, full of pictorial charm and, for Bologna, a new pictorial tradition, but a decisive step toward the new classic feeling has not yet been taken. Nevertheless it is interesting to set one or two mannerist examples of the same theme alongside this *Baptism* of Annibale. Let us then compare the treatment of this subject at the hands of a typical Florentine mannerist, Jacopino del Conte (San Giovanni Decollato, 1541, Fig. 20) the better to appreciate Annibale's steps toward a new corporeality and spatiality, attained through the study of Correggio and the Venetians. Obviously the case is quite different when one turns to the *Baptism* of Santi di Tito (Galleria Corsini, Fig. 21), dating perhaps ten years earlier than Annibale's picture. For in this picture much of what the anti-mannerist movement was striving for has already been achieved, especially the infinitely greater simplicity. In Annibale's painting the heavenly regions, with God the Father and the concert of angels, take up just as much room as the real scene of the Baptism in the Jordan. But in Santi di Tito only the latter is represented, and is confined to relatively few figures at that. The pageantry of angels is not in evidence, and only a bright glow in the midst of dark clouds stands for the supernatural. Here, therefore, Santi di Tito is much more advanced than the young Annibale, paradoxically because his role within late Mannerism is generally conservative. Since his artistic powers were not great enough, however, he never became the initiator of a new style.[9]

Annibale's well-known *Assumption of the Virgin* of 1587 (Dresden, Gemäldegalerie, Fig. 23) is "new" to a much greater extent and is quite distinct from everything manneristic. The picture is surprising on the one hand for its great freshness, and on the other for its remarkably solid, almost awkward, heaviness. The influence of Titian, especially of his world famous Academy picture, is naturally recognizable—as in the attempt to relate the earthly figures to the heavenly ones, but in Annibale the bonds are more tightly drawn. The heavier, more matronly Madonna does not fly upward, nor does she stand on the clouds or soar above them. Rather she glides with outstretched arms close above the heads of the apostles so that she comes into close contact with them. The apostles too are much more heavily earthly than in Titian or even in Mannerism. The construction of such a figure as the apostle seen in profile in the foreground, although thoroughly corporeal and plastic, with its broadly conceived areas of light and shade and its coarse lively features, lies upon the road which Caravaggio, and following him, Rubens, were soon to tread. What is both striking and novel is the way in which these realistic figures are placed in classic or classicizing stage setting. There is a carved sarcophagus in the foreground, columns at the left, and a smaller hall with columns (a kind of grave monument) to the right in the middleground. This static

---

[9] Santi di Tito's rather impressive *Nativity* in San Giuseppe in Florence (Fig. 22), painted according to Baldinucci as early as 1564, puts the question before the spectator: is this a conscious resumption of the Renaissance ideal of Raphael's or Peruzzi's, or is it the continuation of a similar academic undercurrent which never died out? In any case the picture, which reveals definitely realistic and portrait-like traits, particularly in the figure of Joseph (something very similar can be seen in Lodovico's *Birth of John the Baptist* from the year 1600), is not unimportant, and its creator should not be overlooked in the history of the creation of the new style.

setting is admittedly not yet completely clear and intelligible as space. We are aware that this is a first attempt and that the whole problem has not been mastered. But the desire for a stronger unity and for a clearly comprehensible view is apparent. The denser pigmentation, the individualization of the types, and added to this the creation of a circumscribed theatrical stage with a moderate illusion of near-by space, all serve the same purpose—a clearer visual realization. Compare it with other representations of the *Assumption* by Bolognese *maniera* artists (like that by Tiburtio Passerotti in Santa Maria della Purificazione, or Prospero Fontana's overstuffed *Assumption* in the Brera), most of which are completely frozen in an indifferent scheme, wherein upper and lower, heavenly and earthly, remain unrelated. The only similar down-to-earth conception of Mary's appearance is to be found in Federigo Barocci's work, for instance in his *Madonna del Popolo,* who has matronly features similar to Annibale's Madonna. But Barocci's glamour, his soft *sfumato,* and especially the shimmering lacquer tones that distinguish all of his pictures, make him very different from Annibale's ponderous gravity.

Annibale is even more characteristic for our period in another picture, in which he is already approaching his classical (or classicizing) maturity (Palazzo Pitti, Fig. 24). Again there is a union of the earthly and the universal. Christ is enthroned on a cloud, his arms opened wide before a semicircular gloriole, Peter and John on either side. But just below the heavenly region, almost touching the clouds, are St. Hermengild and the Magdalen; and to the right is St. Edward (who often helps cripples, hence the remarkable crawling figure in the center background), who entreats heavenly grace for his protégé Odoardo Farnese. It is characteristic of the new movement that the Carracci were opposed on principle to the inclusion of donor figures in their religious pictures, because they destroy the unified character of the work. But in this case the donor is necessary to the picture's coherence; everything is related to him, even though he himself is modestly backed into a corner.

A picture of such clarity, with such "living" figures and with such intimacy of religious feeling enveloping the heavenly figures in the clouds as well as the saints and the donor on earth, had not been created since the time of the High Renaissance. Make a comparison with the earlier Bolognese master, Orazio Samacchini. In his picture in San Paolo (painted about 1570, Fig. 25), as in Annibale's, the heavens open, Christ appears surrounded by angels with Mary and John kneeling on clouds; and below are Saints Martin and Petronius, the latter the patron of Bologna, whose image with the Asinelli towers appears in the same spot as the portrait of Odoardo in Annibale's picture. In Samacchini the landscape is only a background suggestion, while in Annibale the new landscape development, of which he was the leader, is hallmarked by the atmospheric treatment, as well as by the orderly recession of tectonic layers of hills and the building (St. Peter's). The landscape, however, is only the result of the structure as a whole, which is demonstrably based on thoroughly classical principles; there is the foreground, or scene of action, with its four closely observed "actors"; then, the middleground with the realistic figure of the cripple; and, finally, the background with landscape and buildings. Above this scene, the divinities are deployed in a broad band close to the foreground (not, as in Samacchini, receding into a funnel-like distance). The classical *Christus Triumphator* has risen again. Without the influence of the Roman High Renaissance a new conception such as this would be unimaginable. In this instance, in fact, one can point to a direct relationship; the ancestor of our picture is the so-called "Five Saints" of the Raphael school (perhaps by Penni).[10] It is quite possible that this picture was in Parma (San Paolo) when Annibale was there (Scaramuccia, in 1674, mentions its presence there), and if so he must have studied it thoroughly. The general plan is exactly the same, but to it Annibale has added a good dose of Correggio, with the result that, compared with its stiff, severe, Raphaelesque model, his picture is much more fluid

[10] See Aldo Foratti, *I Carracci* (Città di Castello, 1913), p. 225.

and more attractive in coloring. However the classicizing tendency is even more pronounced and characteristic (especially in the system of layers in the lower part of the picture) than in the "Five Saints." In short, we are dealing in this instance with a transitional work; Annibale no longer gets his inspiration exclusively from north Italian art, but stepping over Mannerism, he reaches back to the classically constructed art of the High Renaissance. The picture must have been painted right at the beginning of his employment by the Farnese, and would thus date shortly after 1595. Soon thereafter, in the last years of the *cinquecento,* Annibale created his most important and most famous work, the decorations of the Farnese Gallery in Rome, for which he was better equipped than any other painter through his earlier experience in decorating Bolognese palaces. Even here, however, he makes not the remotest use of Mannerism's ornamental or decorative elements. In the religious paintings of his late period he attains a truly monumental greatness without a trace of linear formalism. Of his many apotheoses of the Virgin, the last, in Santa Maria del Popolo (Cerasi Chapel, before 1601), is the strongest. As certain early *cinquecento* Assumptions (e.g., Sodoma's in San Bernardino, Siena), the Madonna supported by angels rises direct from the sarcophagus; she is more closely connected or at least structurally more integrated with the earthling group of apostles than in the earlier picture, and for this the vision is all the more gripping. More than ever before, the miracle is humanized—arises, so to speak, from humanity itself, in contrast to the abstract remoteness of Mannerism.

This same shifting of principles may be observed, with variations according to the individual and the locality, among the rest of the painters whom we would like to include in this series of "reformers," along with the well-known Carracci. When they represent scenes, such as the Assumption of the Virgin, or the Ascension of Christ, in which heaven and earth, the divine and the temporal meet, the tendency is the same. Since, however, we will not be able to find outstanding examples of identical religious themes in each case, we shall have to treat some of these men in a different context. Thus, for example, Cigoli's *Resurrection* in Arezzo (1591) is strongly inclined toward Mannerism (partly modeled on Pontormo): for Cardi, called Cigoli, deviated but slowly from the path in which his teacher Alessandro Allori had led him. To be sure his other teacher, Santi di Tito, counterbalanced this influence. Cigoli vacillated a while, but in the end he turned his back definitively upon everything manneristic and became a staunch member of the rational reform movement. His *Descent from the Cross* painted for Empoli (now in the Pitti), which is so important for the history of art, makes this perfectly clear. It is even more pointed in his later works, such as the *Ecce Homo*.

Among the younger men of this group Giovanni Battista Crespi, known as Cerano, deserves attention. As one might expect, the direction of his reform reflects the conditions of his own local school, and is therefore neither Tuscan nor Bolognese but Lombard in overtone. He was the leader of the new generation in Milan.[11] He too was swept along in the new trend toward realism, but even in his late works one can point out certain *retardataire* elements that are left over from Mannerism. Nevertheless what seems to me more important and significant is the fine quality of his beautiful large Madonna pictures (e.g., Uffizi, Fig. 26, and Brera; also the *Madonna del Celso* with the Madonna statue by Fontana in Turin), which are distinguished for their great simplicity, the symmetry of their composition, as well as for the solidity of the forms, and the richness of the coloristic treatment.[12] Just

[11] To which Giulio Cesare Procaccini also belongs; he collaborated with Cerano on some works, including the Borromeo pictures in the cathedral of Milan. He is more strongly Correggesque than his contemporary. For more about him, see Nikolaus Pevsner, "Giulio Cesare Procaccini" in *Rivista d'arte,* XI (1929), pp. 321–54.

[12] On this point I find myself in some degree of disagreement with the views expressed in the otherwise very useful essay by Pevsner on "Die Gemaelde des Giovanni Battista Crespi genannt Ceranno" in the *Jahrbuch der preussischen Kunstsammlungen* (Berlin, 1925), XLVI, 259–85.

like the Carracci and the others, each in his own way, Cerano bases
his style on the pre-mannerists of his native Lombardy, particularly
upon the forms—firm, noble, and uncluttered—of Moretto, to
whom Caravaggio too owed so much. Pordenone also influenced
him.[13] The latter had worked in Cremona and Piacenza, and is not
to be overlooked in tracing the development of the new style in
Lombardy. In order to appreciate the preponderance of the "new
trend" in Cerano's paintings, it is only necessary to compare them
with the oft encountered pictures of a typical Lombard mannerist,
G. B. Trotti. Fundamentally the difference is the same as between
the Carracci and Samacchini, and the like, only that the local flavor
is distinct. Hence Cerano too is one of the "new men," a reformer,
as many more of his pictures (especially the San Carlo Borromeo
series in Milan Cathedral) demonstrate.

There remains Caravaggio. The transcendental, the mystic, the
ecstatic were even more foreign to his nature than to the others—
that much is well known. Nevertheless he could not completely
ignore the demands of his ecclesiastical patrons, and it is interesting
to see how he manages the problem of "real-izing" the transcendental and the holy raised to the sphere of the ideal. The winged
angel in his early *Flight into Egypt,* in spite of its close relation to
Lotto, has a manneristic ring; the same sort of figure in his middle
period (the Berlin *Saint Matthew*) has become a sturdy, buxom,
young woman. He depicts the Magdalen as though she were a sad
little courtesan in a genre scene, and so on.[14] Accordingly one can
hardly speak of "the opening heavens" in his case (in the literal
sense too, the sky hardly ever appears in his works). The only
indication that an upper region exists is in the downward swoop-
ing angel, who makes his appearance in many of Caravaggio's pictures, and always in much the same form. Typical, among others,

[13] For instance, the women on the steps in Cerano's picture in the cathedral of
the *Divisions of the Possessions of San Carlo Borromeo* can be compared with
the women in the *Birth of the Virgin* by Pordenone in Piacenza.

[14] This irritated Francesco Scanelli, *Microcosmo* (Forli, 1647), p. 277, very
much; he confronted the picture with Correggio's *Magdalene.*

are the angels in the big *Martyrdom of Saint Matthew,* in the *Seven Works of Charity* in Naples, and in the *Nativity* in Palermo. But the presence of this angel as a symbol of the transcendental is really nothing but a concession. Even if Caravaggio (as in the case of this angel figure) borrows from Michelangelo [15] and makes use of the static compositional structure of the High Renaissance in his larger picture, his roots are in the realism of his Lombard forefathers. In his choice of motifs especially, but also in other ways, he carries this realism to extremes for the sake of bringing the miraculous as close to earth as possible—sometimes, indeed, so close that it all but vanishes.

HAVING attempted to characterize each of the leading artists of the new movement according to the spiritual as well as the formal tendencies revealed in selected examples of their work, we shall now proceed to a systematic examination of various themes and their characteristic development.

The conversion of St. Paul was a favorite theme of the sixteenth century. The precise time limitation of the visionary moment (i.e., the fall of the saint from horseback when he sees the supernatural apparition—or rather, when he hears a Divine voice) was bound to have special appeal to a style with pronounced spiritual tendencies, such as Mannerism was in the beginning. Its formal possibilities, too, are well suited to Mannerism, as it is full of opportunities for the depiction of large, violently agitated groups, tumult, overlapping bodies, and so on. Raphael's tapestry cartoon, with the saint lying in the foreground while the horse gallops off into the distance and Christ appears above, was well known, of course (Fig. 27).[16] Even more famous was Michelangelo's mag-

---

[15] The attitude of the torso, the head and the arms of the figure, are reminiscent of the angel on the left side of the *Last Judgment,* who is pulling up one of the Elect.

[16] The representation of the *Conversion of St. Paul* on the left side of the large painting devoted to St. Paul by Domenico Beccafumi (1515, Siena) is also

nificent version of the subject in the Cappella Paolina, dating from the 1540s (Fig. 28). Here the fleeing horse in the center is flanked by agitated groups to the left and right, while above floats the heavenly host, from whose midst Christ rushes in headlong descent. Even Michelangelo's composition, however, served as inspiration in detail rather than as a whole. Salviati's contemporaneous, but quite independent, version of the subject in the Galleria Doria may serve as a typical mannerist example (Fig. 29). Here the emphasis is placed upon the melée in the middle, whose focal point is the figure of the saint, prostrated by the blinding apparition. However, the groups of tangled men and horses on either side are given almost as much importance in the composition. The vision itself is not given much room. Christ appears among clouds, over a glimpse of landscape. The elder Zuccaro (Taddeo), in his impressive picture in San Marcello al Corso (ca. 1560), borrows Salviati's motif of the saint thrown backwards with one leg still engaged in the saddle. The rising figure comes from Michelangelo, but aside from these he has nothing to do with either of them. The figures in the Zuccaro picture have become even more tangled and interlaced. Christ appears, pointing downward (as in Michelangelo), fairly close to the front alone.

In Bologna we find a *Conversion* by Ercole Procaccini, the eldest of the family, in the church of San Giacomo Maggiore, painted in 1543 (Fig. 30). St. Paul, in a somewhat Michelangelesque pose, is stretched out in the foreground, his left leg supported against the horse (as in Michelangelo and Zuccaro) lying obliquely behind him. His face is raised to the vision in the clouds above. Warriors, some of them mounted, are running off to both sides in the middle-ground. The tall, tightly compressed composition is built along crossed diagonals leading into the picture, but the effect nevertheless is one of flatness. The fallen saint is depicted in much the same

---

highly original. The horse is not to be seen, the stricken St. Paul lies in the foreground as though in a trance, and behind him there are some warriors standing and gesticulating. The apparition is at the very top, in the clouds.

pose and with similar expression in a drawing by Denis Calvaert dated 1579 (Louvre; Fig. 31), which was used, with some variations, for the picture (Fig. 32) in a Viennese private collection. Christ speaks, as is customary, out of the clouds; the warriors protect themselves from the blinding light of the supernatural apparition by hiding behind their shields (the motif occurs uniquely in the drawing). The horse is placed to one side in the background, rearing. Lodovico is then set off against the background of these predecessors about 1584–89. He adapts the motive of the figure who reclines in the foreground half raising himself and gazing upwards, but he transforms the pallid mannerist figure into a man of flesh and blood (Fig. 33). The saint (as in Raphael and Michelangelo) has fallen clear of the horse, though the latter is very much in evidence. Unlike the fallen horses of the mannerist pictures, it rears up, foreshortened (though not as sharply as in Michelangelo), and extends diagonally into the picture. This, in conjunction with the bodily contortion of the saint, brings about considerable projection into the depth. Over, or between, the still somewhat disorderly figures of the companions there is created a kind of funnel into the picture space (a device that Lodovico uses in other pictures as well), terminating in a landscape with a bridge. It is significant that in the striated sky with bright areas left by the parting clouds there is nowhere visible the usual incarnate vision. There is shown no Christ, nor hosts of angels, only an expanse of brilliant light. The bemused and ecstatic Saul–Paul gazes into this bright spot, the cause of his misadventure, for it is thence that the words of Jesus echo forth: "Saul, Saul, wherefore dost thou persecute me?" His companions too, as stated in the text, hear the voice but see nobody. Here, then, the vision is only implied through its visible consequences on its human recipients.[17]

[17] It has been brought to my attention and confirmed by the Soprintendenza in Bologna that there is, in the upper right hand corner of the painting, a figure of Christ which is scarcely visible and only sketched in monochrome. Possibly this is a later addition; in any case this does not change the tenor of the very large painting.

By far the most radical treatment of the *Conversion of St. Paul* is Caravaggio's. In his magnificent painting in the Cerasi Chapel (ca. 1600, Fig. 34) there is no place left at all for visions. The great horse and the old man at its head (probably inspired by Dürer's engraving of 1505) fill the entire background of the picture, blocking the view of sky and everything else. In front, but isolated from them, lies the extremely foreshortened (cf. Zuccaro, *et al*) figure of St. Paul. His arms are outstretched, his eyes closed, as in the Biblical text (as also in some other pictures, such as Zuccaro's). The picture is extraordinarily powerful and impressive. The miracle is taking place inside of a single individual, and it is only through its pathological effects on him that the spectator is aware of it.[18]

The theme of "Christ and the apostles at Emmaus"—a lesser "Last Supper"—had met with but small favor among the real mannerists. Three days after the Crucifixion, Christ appeared to two of His apostles on their way to Emmaus, and when He broke bread for them after their arrival at the inn, He was recognized by this gesture. The simplicity of the theme, which offers no pretext for the violent movement and ornamental interplay beloved of Mannerism, probably held little attraction for the mannerist temper. Neither was there much demand for depictions of the scene from ecclesiastical quarters, because it is so similar to the Last Supper. Until the High Renaissance it seldom appears as an independent scene, but usually only as part of the Passion sequence. In the *cinquecento,* however, it steps forward as an entity, especially among the Venetian artists—Bellini, Titian, Moretto, and Veronese —and again during the antimannerist movement at the end of the century it is popular with the painters who turned for inspiration to the Venetian High Renaissance. The simplicity of the theme, with its mystical content, gave the subject high value also in the Northern countries. The pinnacle of its development can be found in Rembrandt's Louvre picture.

[18] The four paragraphs above have been added to the original German text.

Pontormo's *Supper at Emmaus* (1528, which is distinctly related, in its composition, to Dürer's rendition of the scene in the *Small Passion*) is the only example that I know of by an early mannerist. As is usual in Pontormo's work, the abstract and the spiritual are emphasized in his rapt attenuated figures. The eye of God, enframed by the triangle and an auriole, floats above the head of the Divinity, and behind the table on either side of Christ there are several other agitated, ecstatic figures. The Venetian examples are quite different. Although Veronese in his Louvre picture enriches the scene, as is his wont, with a herd of secular figures, men, women, and children, it is Titian's solemnly beautiful version (Louvre, ca. 1540) that engages our attention. Its special effectiveness is due to the broad expanse of white tablecloth, and to the reduction in the number of figures to include only Christ, the two apostles, the innkeeper, and the young servant. Moretto's *Supper* in Brescia (also ca. 1540) is related to it, but even further simplified.[19] Here everything is concentrated upon the climactic moment when the apostles recognize Our Lord as He breaks the bread (only to lose Him again immediately: Luke: 24, 31).

In Florence I can cite only a picture by Cigoli (or his school) in the Pitti, which approaches the painting of Veronese in having secondary figures participate in the action to a greater extent than usual. Caravaggio's representation of the scene is much more important and characteristic. It derives from the north Italian way of handling the scene, as seen in Titian and Moretto (for Brescia was close to Caravaggio artistically as well as being near his birthplace). Two versions exist, both mentioned by Bellori. The simpler is the one owned by the Marchese Patrizi (Fig. 35). Christ's gesture is the same as in the Titian, His right hand is raised, and before Him on the table lies the bread, already broken. The placing of the innkeeper, who stands behind the table between Christ and one of the disciples, is similar to the Titian. An old woman is present. The two disciples, moved closer to Christ, as in Moretto,

---

[19] There is a drawing for it in the Print Room at Copenhagen.

show the same movements of astonishment. One of them also recalls, in type, the disciple on the left in Moretto. In the version in London (Fig. 36), the bread is somewhat covered by the benedictory hand, and hence does not play so important a role. On the other hand the gesture is much more vivid—it is a revelation, and is manifested as such by the expansive gestures of the disciples, especially the bearded one on the right. The innkeeper is more in the shadow, the wrinkled old woman has disappeared, and accordingly the still life on the table is richer. In any event, in both versions the emancipation from everything manneristic is decisive, and here once again this has been accomplished by relying upon the post-classical models of a still earlier generation, to which Moretto also belongs in every respect. Hence in Caravaggio too there emerges a new inward spirituality, accompanying the emphasis he places on the plastic, corporeal, and realistic values. The miracle of the apparition of Christ has become human, it might almost be said, Protestant.

IT is important, too, that the visions of the saints were also now humanized. The saints themselves took on even a homely character, giving rise to a special kind of inwardness. The most important visionary saint and at the same time the most human, St. Francis, whose stigmatization is encountered relatively seldom in the Italian *quattrocento* and High Renaissance, again comes to the fore in the second half of the sixteenth century. It is worth noticing, however, that he does not appear in Mannerism proper, to which "Gothicizing" tendencies can otherwise be attributed, but in that important, though secondary, trend which is represented by Federigo Barocci, then continues in the Bolognese, and appears to a very marked degree in the Florentine, Cigoli.[20]

[20] This phenomenon is connected with the history of the Franciscan order, whose decline in the fourteenth and fifteenth centuries reached its culminating point in the rift of the order in 1515. Then the branch of strict "Observants" began to flourish again, in a peculiar way starting from single centers, the so-called

Barocci is the creator of those figures, which in spite of their ecstatic rapture, never, or seldom, take on anormative form or bodily attentuation and twisting. Rather they almost always preserve a healthy corporeality having an immediate relation to the atmosphere, to mountain, tree, castle, cloud, and air. This is shown by his *Beata Michelina* (Fig. 37), in which the enraptured Franciscan nun kneels upon a hill before the visionary apparition of light which breaks through the flying clouds. She is completely enveloped in the air and wind, in the atmosphere of the bright and mysterious moonlit night, and yet thereby keeps her sturdy and substantial womanly character. (The same is true of St. Dominic in the *Madonna della Rosario* in Sinigaglia.) Barocci's representations of St. Francis are created in this same spirit. The study in Florence (Fig. 38) is striking, particularly in its light effects. A heavenly light strikes St. Francis, dazzles Father Rufinus, who is lying in the foreground with his right hand shielding his eyes, and clearly illuminates the rustic landscape background. Cigoli, who made innumerable pictures of St. Francis, followed in Barocci's path. Although he is Barocci's inferior as a painter, he communicates to a greater degree the physiognomic and inward qualities. In one series of his compositions St. Francis is shown painfully enraptured, receiving the stigmata in a rocky landscape with the apparition blazing, and the *portiuncula* in the background (Fig. 39) seemingly in continuation of Barocci. But in a second

"ritiros." (This was similar to what had happened in Spain by means of the Discalceatos under Petrus of Alcantara, and probably influenced thereby.) This movement, the "Observants of St. Francis," spread particularly from middle Italy, from the valley of Rieti, and this may have provided the impetus for Barocci's representations of St. Francis in nearby Urbino. The sporadic appearance of the vision of St. Francis in the art of the later *cinquecento* can also be explained by the influence of these dispersed "ritiros." The new cult of St. Francis may have reached Bologna and the Carracci through the Bolognese pope, Gregory XIII, who patronized the Franciscan "Observants" and the "Reformatos of the Ritiros" at the end of the seventies. Similar influences may also have played a role in Cigoli's production of St. Francis pictures, for toward the end of the nineties Clement VIII was a great encourager of Franciscan efforts.

series he shows the saint quietly kneeling in prayer, in such a way that a distinctive portrait-like quality comes strongly to the fore (Fig. 40). This emphasis on characterization also finds expression in the work of the Carracci, who also painted St. Francis often and with pleasure. Agostino's picture in Vienna displays the very skillful draftsmanship for which he is known, but it is prosaic. By contrast, in Lodovico, the personality of the saint is very vivid and full of physiognomic insight. As an example I would cite the *Madonna del Rosario* in Bologna (Pinacoteca, Fig. 41), where the intimate human relationship of St. Francis to the Madonna and Child is especially sympathetic. There is also a portrait-like study of St. Francis in Turin, which is either by Cerano or someone close to him.

The change to the actual and normative manifests itself in the religious and transcendental realm, and particularly in the much favored devotional pictures, the representations of the saints, who are rendered as portraits of individuals, although ones who are subject to visions. Lodovico Carracci shows the martyrdom of St. Pietro Toma (according to others it is a St. Angelo), who was fastened to a tree as though to a crucifix. In his hands it becomes a vision that could almost be said to be after life (Fig. 42). In his formerly very famous St. Hyacinthus, as the saint kneels before the altar, an angel shows him an inscribed tablet, while above the Madonna and angels appear in the sky, as though before his inward eye. The figure of Hyacinthus is not at all a mere cliché, but rather gives the effect of being completely an individual (Louvre, 1594, Fig. 43). This is even more true of the highly expressive face of St. Charles Borromeo, who was often painted as a saint even before his canonization, which did not occur until 1610. In a picture in San Bartolommeo in Bologna (Fig. 44), Lodovico depicts him as he kneels before the empty sarcophagus in Varallo in the presence of an angel. We naturally encounter St. Charles most frequently in the place where he still lived in personal memory, in Milan, especially during the time that his nephew Federigo was

Bishop of Milan, and a sponsor of the arts and learning as well. So it is natural that Cerano, his favorite painter, should have represented St. Charles very often—in the act of devotion, for example, as in the handsome painting in the Certosa of Pavia and elsewhere. The picture shows the enthroned Madonna with St. Charles and St. Ambrose (Fig. 45), and reveals, in its simplicity and characteristic corporeality, how very much Cerano belonged to the new generation. The continuation of this trend may be seen in Daniele Crespi's picture of St. Charles at his frugal meal reading the Gospel and weeping over the Passion of Christ (Fig. 46). In this instance too, the subject is fundamentally a vision; it is just that it has been completely relegated to the individual psyche.[21]

IF we gather together the various results which may be drawn from the production of those artists who were at the height of their careers between 1590 and 1600, there is nothing identical, because the artistic individualities are too different, but there is at least something related in their general tendency. From the negative point of view there is a turning away from Mannerism and the *maniera*. From the positive, there is a reform moving in the direc-

---

[21] The secular activities of the saint were also represented by preference about 1600 in Milan, not only because St. Charles was particularly close to the Milanese in time, but even more so because of the completely new realistic attitude of the period. This is clearly shown in the large paintings by Cerano and his collaborators (Procaccini, etc.) which are now preserved in the cathedral of Milan and only shown at the festival of St. Charles at the beginning of November. They represent the miraculous deeds of St. Charles, such as his healing of the goldsmith's wife; but other exploits of the new saint are even more remarkable, such as the scene in which he distributed his possessions or the consecration of the crosses, for here the worldly and physical, the realistic and opulent, come strongly to the fore, going back beyond the manneristic period and tendencies to the preceding brilliant period of Venetian art—in this case, I believe, upon Pordenone, particularly his frescoes in nearby Piacenza. The way in which in Cerano's painting the women rush up the stairs to the treasures which are to be distributed and the way in which the nobles converse, reveal an almost Shakespearian revival of a strong, realistic, and assured artistic sentiment.

tion of the actual, the normative and reasonable, the human and the inward, and going forward by means of a contact with the prototypes of the Italian "classical" period, those from the flowering of north Italian art in Parma and the Veneto, rather more than the Roman. In this way a new situation was also created for the transcendental, apotheosistic, the visionary and miraculous. The quality of the ecstatic in the expressive formulation of early Mannerism, in Pontormo, Rosso, and partly Parmigianino, disappears, or is definitely lessened. And the formulae of the *maniera* artists, too, their allegorical and far-fetched way of handling religious themes, is also for the most part abandoned. The new spiritual approach demanded poise and quiet in dealing with the deepest tumults of the human soul, just as it did in dealing with visions. We have seen how an attempt was made even to transpose miracles wholly into the soul of man, and how too, even in the case of the saints, the qualities of individuality and psychological penetration were more and more valued.

The secularization of the transcendental, as we see it emerge in the art of the waning sixteenth century, naturally does not at all suppose any diminution in religious feeling. On the contrary, when previously the supernatural had been set apart in a restricted zone into which only an ecstatic, a man transported, could penetrate, the holy realm was made distant from the human, and to a certain degree schematized. The two realms, the world on the one hand, and the vision on the other, were thus somewhat divided, and linked to each other only by the "credo quia absurdum," by the sight of the invisible. Like the Middle Ages, the spirituality of the manneristic epoch could grasp the supernatural, the divine and visionary, only in this way. Artistically this spirituality stressed as a whole the greatest possible abstraction, of line, of the body, and of space, that is to say, a complete detachment, or at least the greatest possible separation from the material and the real. So even more when it came to the representation of supernatural themes, Mannerism sought for the most far-reaching removal from everything earthly, for something purely speculative, that had to do with the human norm only just so far as was necessary to remain comprehensible. In this way Mannerism decisively separated itself from the Renaissance, which, like classical antiquity, saw in the supernatural only a heightened form of the human. But if the humanizing process is carried still farther, if the religious element is transposed into the realm of the existing and actual, then the distance between them is abolished and religion comes close to the world, though in a different sense from the Renaissance. Worldly things are then permeated with religion, with other-worldly aspects. This was exactly the goal toward which the great leaders of the religious orders were striving at this time, the end of the sixteenth century—the Jesuits above all. Reason was not only allowed in the cause of the supernatural, it was even very much encouraged, as long as the sentiment and the faith were sustained, or better, if the proximity of the miracle to the earth lent force to the vision. Hence religious art could well become realistic, as long as it was saturated with religion. Whereas the art of Mannerism proceeded speculatively in the treatment of the supernatural, using symbol and allegory, in the new period, this was thoroughly altered both in form and content, corresponding to the change under way in religious feeling. For both miracles and visions were now placed in man's closest and demonstrable surroundings, or even in his own heart. A new warmth of religious feeling arose, which was immediately convincing because it was immediately understandable. The concreteness of what was represented, attained by the use of all the means which we have mentioned—physical corporeality, density of pigment, nearness of space—was hence in no way contradictory to the depth of religious experience. It was from this new type of feeling that the new art of the post-manneristic epoch drew its deepest justification.

It should not be surprising that this process of transformation took various forms among the individual artists, who were, as has been said, extremely different from each other. Lodovico Carracci, born in 1555, is highly uneven in his production, and not always comprehensible in his development. As one schooled on Correggio and Tintoretto, he is the most emotional and free in his pictures, and he is the foremost as the painter of psychic and religious movement. His tendencies are passed on primarily to the painterly and optical trend of the *seicento*. Quite the opposite is true of his cousin Annibale, five years his junior, who represented the visionary in firm, almost classical, constructions, but without relinquishing the coloristic impressions of his youth in northern Italy. Cigoli, who was almost the same age, separated himself decisively from Florentine linear Mannerism by his dependence on Barocci. Yet his style was never so meltingly soft as Barocci's but preserved something of the general Florentine harshness of local color, which he bequeathed to his followers in the *seicento*. His formulations of St. Francis are important for the new style. Finally the new spiritual orientation comes to fruition in two painters whose birth dates, on the basis of recent research, must be placed somewhat later than was formerly thought, so that they are separated from this first group by ten or fifteen years. One of them is the Milanese Giovanni Battista Crespi, called Cerano. Although he was born around 1575, in many of his pictures Cerano nevertheless appears more manneristic than older men, even after 1600, which may be partly explained by the peripheral location of his artistic activity in the region of Milan. But in his case, too, what is decisive must not be sought in those pictures in which he is still constrained by the old *maniera,* but in the ones that reveal his new feeling for the actual and the material. In his large pictures of the Madonna, as has been indicated, he returns to a simple and yet substantial and materially enhanced form, of which similar early examples were already present in Moretto and other north Italian countrymen of the thirties and forties. It may also be found in the way he represented his favorite saint, St. Charles, in forceful virility sumptuously accomplishing splendid deeds, but nevertheless he managed to characterize him as a visionary. But the most radical, even in the visionary and ecstatic sphere, was Michelangelo da Caravaggio, who likewise stemmed from the Lombard-Venetian masters of the early *cinquecento* (Lotto, Savoldo, etc.) and who was Cerano's compatriot and near contemporary. Caravaggio, by his own completely personal, almost lyrical realism, carried the process of humanization to its highest point, and with it, in the most literal sense, the lodging of the miracle within the human heart.

A question may now be formulated. This was an art which these men, with whom can be grouped a whole series of lesser or ineffectual personalities, produced in opposition to the ideals of their immediate predecessors. It was one that despite strong individual differences and opposed principles manifested, nevertheless, a unified and sharply distinctive trend, particularly in the representation of the transcendental, as we have tried to show. Can this art be equated with what is commonly called Baroque? Is it one kind of Baroque or even *the* Baroque? Approached as a question of semantics, we find the same situation here that applies to the expression Mannerism. As I pointed out at the outset, this term was immediately applicable only to the second part of the period, the phase of the *maniera,* and was extended to include the first period by virtue of its being the foundation. Similarly *barocco* was applied as a term of contempt to all that was hated by the rational, classicistic trend toward the end of the *seicento,* and later down to Milizia. It applied to what from the classicistic point of view were the explosive, inflated, extravagant works of a Bernini, a Borromini, or a Pietro da Cortona, to these "pestilential diseases of good taste," but not on any account to the works of the Carracci, particularly Annibale's, which were far rather esteemed as models and as coming of good classical family. Nor was the epithet "baroque" ever bestowed upon Caravaggio, in spite of all his antagonism to the classicistic and idealistic. Here again the art historians of the nineteenth century must be held responsible for causing confusion, placing the beginning of the Baroque in painting around 1580, that is at roughly the time of the building of the Gesù, and contrasting it to the Renaissance. Actually and historically the painting in the period under discussion arose in opposition to the *maniera* of the late *cinquecento,* but not at all to the same degree, nor in antithesis to the so-called High Renaissance. On the contrary, the temper of the generation growing up around 1580 had its spiritual foundation in the painting of the early, or earlier, *cinquecento,* which served as their model and can therefore be called "classic" for them. This fact they never denied, and it has been pointed out repeatedly here. Hence it would be more correct to call this time of reform, or healthful recovery and realization, a neo-classical or neo-Renaissance period, although then there would be the danger, always present with such terms, that associations slip in which becloud scientific understanding, and if it were not also for the fact that the differences from the outlook of the actual Renaissance were still very considerable, as has just been shown in the realm of religion. For it cannot be denied that the period around 1590 or 1600 was, in spite of its retrospective ties, thoroughly *sui generis,* thoroughly original, and that is the root of its surpassing historical importance. Probably we should use a somewhat colorless, noncommittal name, which merely indicates the limits, post or antimanneristic, or looking to the future, early, or rather pre-Baroque. It would be best if all these terms such as Gothic, Renaissance, Mannerism, Baroque, Classicism, and so forth, which were apparently willfully promulgated and defined, were only used when they meant something very definite and circumscribed. In any case a period should always be restricted to one or two generations, and not used to include completely different trends under a common denominator like "The Art of the Baroque."

Naturally many threads led into the future from this period of the "reformers"—the period of the Carracci, Cigoli, Caravaggio, and Cerano—which did not last more than thirty years. We have already referred to Lodovico as the precursor of an optically dissolved trend within the Baroque, and Annibale and his pupils are claimed by the whole classical current of the seventeenth century.

Florentine *seicento* men like Biliverti, Cristofano Allori, and so forth claim Cigoli. The realists and "tenebrosi" of Italy, Spain, and the Netherlands claim Caravaggio. It is not my purpose here to go into the new spiritual transformation that occurred in the second or third decade of the seventeenth century, nor its effect upon the painting of the transcendental, particularly upon the properly Baroque painting of visions and ecstasy. For these, if one thinks, for instance, of Bernini's work as a sculptor, are essentially different from our period.

IN conclusion I should like to refer to a northern artist who surpassed all the Italian artists of this period, even Caravaggio, in quality and strength of perception. I am referring to Peter Paul Rubens. In so far as his age was concerned, he did not belong to this generation, for he was seventeen years younger than Annibale, and four years younger than Caravaggio, but when he went to Italy in 1600 the work of these masters was the most modern then to be seen. The mannerists were at this time a superannuated and vanquished trend, and accordingly very few artistic connections to them can be seen in Rubens' work (except for what may have filtered in through his teacher Van Veen). His predilection for Caravaggio's art is well known, and although he did not become a Caravaggist, he even negotiated the sale of some of his pictures.

But he also studied the Carracci very carefully, not only Annibale, who was more in his own artistic line, but also Lodovico.[22] In Cerano's beautiful Madonna in the Uffizi at least the strongly glowing and modern treatment of the color is strikingly related to Rubens' conception of color at this time. And finally there also exist direct and demonstrable relations between Rubens and the Florentine circle of reformers, especially Cigoli. It is true that in the fea-

[22] Riegl, *Entstehung,* 169, says speaking of the St. Jerome on the left side of Lodovico's *Madonna degli Scalzi:* "Here is where Rubens derived the inspiration for his splendid male type."

tures he borrowed and the stimuli which he undeniably received from this circle of proto-Baroque reformers there was nothing decisive for him. Rather the essential thing in Rubens' art is just the very crescendo with which he surpasses any master. After a relatively short pre-Baroque period, in which these influences were assimilated, his style proceeds to an ever intensified vehemence, of form, of movement, of color and light, that is, it mounts more and more to a high Baroque stage. His representations of transcendental subjects were drawn along in this development—as an example I will cite another *Conversion of St. Paul* (1616) which is composed in wild movement rather than being restrained or inward, and which, without any direct derivation, transposes the representations of a Salviati or a Zuccaro out of mannerist forms into Baroque. The same process goes on in the case of the *Apparition of Christ*. Rubens' saints are no longer characterized as simple human beings, as in Lodovico and Cerano, but in a typically Baroque manner are completely deified in close juxtaposition to an opened heaven and hordes of angels. (Cf. the *Miracle of St. Francis Xavier,* 1619–1620.) The same thing is true of the apotheosis. The divine is not made human, but rather the two extremes approach in another way; Man becomes God, and the apotheosis takes on its ancient meaning, in the *Wedding of Henry IV* in the Medici cycle, as well as in the sketch for the Whitehall *Happy Reign of James I*. The Kingly Man, and God, are one. This is an ultimate extension but also a reversal of the relation between God and man as it was laid down during the period of reform around 1590.

INDEX

Academies, influence of, 52-53

Allegory in anti-Mannerism, 57, 58

Allori, Alessandro, 51, 66

Apotheosis of the Virgin (Annibale Carracci, in Santa Maria del Popolo), 65

Apparition of Christ (Rubens), 83

Appearance, form of, 6-7

Architecture, Mannerism and, 9, 9*n*, 14

Art theory, 53

Assumption of the Virgin (Annibale Carracci), 62-63

Assumption of the Virgin (Rosso Fiorentino), 28

Assumption of the Virgin (Titian), 28

Augustus and the Sibyl (Peruzzi), 19

Baptism of Christ (Annibale Carracci), 61-62

Baptism of Christ (del Conte), 61

Baptism of Christ (Santi di Tito), 61

Barocci, Federigo, 50, 63, 74

Baroque Art, Renaissance influence on, 11; in Lodovico Carracci, 60; term, 80-81

Bathhouse (Dürer), 27

Beata Michelina (Barocci), 74

Beauty, new concept of, in Mannerism, 8

Beccafumi, Domenico, 42*n*

Bolognese School, 56, 74*n*

Bronzino, 41

Calvaert, Denis (*Conversion of St. Paul*), 69-70

Campi, Giulio, 51

Cappella Paolina (Rome), Michelangelo's frescoes in, 14, 18, 68-69

Caravaggio, Michelangelo da, 67-68; anti-mannerist reforms, 51; cultural background, 53; *Conversion of St. Paul,* 71; *Supper at Emmaus,* 72-73; process of humanization in, 80; Rubens and, 82

Carracci, Agostino: cultural background, 53; *Communion of St. Jerome,* 60; representation of St. Francis, 75

Carracci, Annibale, 60-65; cultural background, 53; transcendental themes treatment, 60-61; color treatment, 61; *Assumption of the Virgin,* 62; decorations for Farnese Gallery, 65; characteristics of, 79; precursor of Baroque, 81

Carracci, Lodovico, 55-60; cultural background, 53; *Madonna degli Scalzi,* 55-56, 57, 58; color treatment, 58*n*; *Transfiguration,* 59-60; treat-

Carracci, Lodovico (*Continued*) ment of theme of Conversion of St. Paul, 70; representation of saints, 75; as painter of psychic and religious movement, 78-79; precursor of Baroque, 81

Carracci circle, the, 51, 58

Carrying of the Cross (Pontormo), 24

Cerano (Giovanni Battista Crespi), 66-67; as anti-mannerist reformer, 51; cultural background, 53; representation of St. Charles Borromeo, 76, 76n, 79; spiritual orientation, 79

Certosa del Galluzzo (Val d'Ema), Pontormo's frescoes, 23-25

Christ and the Apostles at Emmaus, treatment of theme, 71-73

Christ Before Pilate (Pontormo), 24, 27

Christ in Glory (Annibale Carracci), 63-64

Christ in Glory (Samacchini), 64

Cigoli, Lodovico Cardi da: as anti-mannerist reformer, 51; cultural background, 53; *Resurrection,* 66; *Supper at Emmaus,* 72; representation of St. Francis, 74; stylistic characteristics of, 79

Color: Rosso's treatment of, 28, 29, 33, 39; in Parmigianino, 39; in Pontormo, 39; in Lodovico Carracci, 58n

Communion of St. Jerome (Agostino Carracci), 60

Conversion of St. Paul, treatment of theme, 68-71

Conversion of St. Paul (Calvaert), 69-70

Conversion of St. Paul (Caravaggio), 71

Conversion of St. Paul (Lodovico Carracci), 70

Conversion of St. Paul (Michelangelo), 68-69

Conversion of St. Paul (Ercole Procaccini), 69

Conversion of St. Paul (Raphael), 68

Conversion of St. Paul (Rubens), 83

Conversion of St. Paul (Salviati), 69

Coronation of the Virgin (Samacchini), 60

Correggio: influence on Parmigianino, 34, 35n; influence on Lodovico Carracci, 59; Annibale Carracci's relation to, 61

Crescent moon, in representation of Immaculate Conception, 56, 57, 57n, 58

Crespi, Daniele, 76

Crespi, Giovanni Battista, *see* Cerano

Crucifixion (Daniele da Volterra), 19

Crucifixion of St. Peter (Michelangelo), 18

David-Apollo figure (Michelangelo), 13-14

Deposition from the Cross (Filippino Lippi), 30

Deposition from the Cross (Rosso Fiorentino), 29-32

Descent from the Cross (Cigoli), 66

Disegno (design), abstract tendencies in, 9-10

Doni Madonna (Michelangelo), 13, 13n

Dürer, Albrecht, influence on Pontormo, 3-4, 25-27

El Greco, *see* Greco, El

Entombment (Pontormo), 38n

Eurythmy, 7n

Farnese Gallery (Rome), Annibale Carracci's decorations, 65

Flight into Egypt (Caravaggio), 67

Florence: normative attitude of High Renaissance art, 5; aspects and sequence of Mannerism in, 9-10, 41, 47, 48; Michelangelo and Mannerism in, 13; influence of Pontormo's Certosa paintings, 25; relationship between Parmigianino and Florentine Mannerism, 39, 40-41

Fontainebleau School, Rosso's relation to, 41

Fontana, Prospero, 51, 56
Fra Bartolommeo, 4, 5

Gethsemane (Pontormo), 24
Giulio Romano, 19
Gloria (Rosso Fiorentino), 28
Gothic art: Mannerism's approach to, 10, 25; influence in Rosso's *Deposition from the Cross,* 30; Renaissance fight against, 25; influence on Pontormo, 26, 27-28
Greco, El: space solution in, 9; Parmigianino's influence on, 42; Mannerism in, 52n
Guido Reni, 57, 57n

High Renaissance: Pontormo's reaction against, 4; resolution of duality of human figure and space, 4-5; Mannerism's relation to, 11; symmetry in, in contrast to Mannerism, 7; death of Raphael marking end of, 43; influence on anti-mannerist style, 64

Il Moretto, 72
Immaculate Conception, representation of theme, 56-58
Immaculate Conception (Vasari), 56

Jacopino del Conte, 61
Julius Tomb (Michelangelo), 13, 14

Landscape: role in Mannerism, 9; appearance in anti-Mannerism, 58; new development in Annibale Carracci, 64
Last Judgment (Michelangelo), 12, 14, 16-17, 42
Laurentian Library, Michelangelo's Mannerism in anteroom of, 14
Life of Joseph (Pontormo), 27n
Light: Rosso's treatment of, 31, 33; flowing light in Parmigianino, 39; role in Lodovico Carracci, 60
Lombard school, 66-67, 66n, 75-76, 76n
Love Cutting his Bow (Pontormo), 38n
Lyricism in anti-Mannerism, 58

Madonna, Doni (Michelangelo), 13, 13n
Madonna and Child with Saints (Cerano), 66
Madonna and Child with Saints (Pontormo, San Michele Visdomini), 20-21
Madonna Appearing to St. Hyacinth (Lodovico Carracci), 75
Madonna degli Scalzi (Lodovico Carracci), 55-56, 57, 58
Madonna del Popolo (Barocci), 63
Madonna del Rosario (Lodovico Carracci), 75
Madonna Enthroned with Saints (Rosso Fiorentino), 29
Madonna of the Long Neck (Parmigianino), 38
Madonna with St. Charles Borromeo and St. Ambrogio (Cerano), 76
Madonna with St. Sebastian (Correggio), 35n
Madonna with Two Deacons (Parmigianino), 40
Maniera, definition of word, 47-48
Marriage of St. Catherine (Parmigianino), 34-35
Marriage of the Virgin (Rosso Fiorentino), 29
Martyrdom of St. Angelo (Lodovico Carracci), 75
Martyrdom of St. Matthew (Caravaggio), 68
Meal of St. Charles Borromeo, The (Crespi), 76
Medici Chapel, 13, 14, 42
Medici *Madonna* (Michelangelo), 13
Medici Villa (Poggio a Caiano), Pontormo's decorations, 22-23, 22n
Michelangelo, 12-19; Mannerism in architecture, 14; space treatment, 14-18; Pontormo, influence on, 23n; Rosso Fiorentino, influence on, 31, 32; Parmigianino, influence on, 36; influence on establishment of mannerist style, 42; treatment of Conversion of St. Paul, 68-69

Moretto, Il, 72
Moses Defending the Daughters of Jethro (Rosso Fiorentino), 32-34
Murillo, Bartolomé Estebán, 57

Nativity (Caravaggio), 68
Nativity (Santi di Tito), 62

"Optical" art, 10*n*

Parmigianino (Francesco Mazzola), 34-41; Michelangelo's influence on, 36; color treatment, 39; relationship beween Florentine Mannerism and, 39, 40-41; Pontormo and Rosso's influence on, 37, 39-40; influence in northern Italy of, 42
Pauline Chapel, see *Cappella Paolina*
Peruzzi, Baldassare, 19
Pietà (Pontormo), 24
Pietà, Rondanini (Michelangelo), 14
Poggio a Caiano, Pontormo's decorations in Medici Villa, 22-23, 22*n*
Pontormo, Jacopo da, 20-28; Dürer's influence on, 3-4, 25-27; Michelangelo's influence on, 23*n*, 41; frescoes at the Certosa del Galluzzo, 23-25; influence of Gothic art on, 26, 27-28; Parmigianino, influence on, 39; *Supper at Emmaus,* 72; lunette decorations at Medici Villa in Poggio a Caiano, 22-23, 22*n*; drawing in the Uffizi, 22-23, 22*n*
Pordenone, 67
Presentation in the Temple (Peruzzi), 19
Primaticcio, 42
Procaccini, Ercole, 69
Procaccini, Giulio Cesare, 66*n*

Quattrocento: compared to High Rennaissance, 4-5; difference between Mannerism and, 9; signposts of Mannerism in mainstream of, 11

Raphael, 19, 43, 68
Renaissance, 25, 54; *see also* High Renaissance

Resurrection (Cigoli), 66
Resurrection (Pontormo), 24-25
Resurrection (Zuccaro), 60
Rome: Rosso and Parmigianino in, 37, 41; "mannered" style in, 48
Rondanini *Pietà* (Michelangelo), 14
Rosso Fiorentino, 28-34; *Deposition from the Cross,* 29-32; Michelangelo's influence on, 31, 32; *Moses Defending the Daughters of Jethro,* 32-34; Parmigianino, influence on, 37, 39; at Fontainebleau, 41; Lodovico Carracci's *Transfiguration* in relation, to, 59
Rubens, Peter Paul, 82-83

St. Charles Borromeo, representation of, 75-76, 76*n*, 79
St. Charles Borromeo before the Sarcophagus, (Lodovico Carracci), 75
St. Francis, representation of, 73-74, 74*n*
St. Francis in Prayer (Cigoli), 74
St. George (Parmigianino), 35
St. John the Evangelist (Pontormo), 27*n*-28*n*
St. Hyacinthus, representation of (Lodovico Carracci), 75
St. Matthew (Caravaggio), 67
St. Michelina (Barocci), 74
St. Paul, Conversion of, treatment of theme, 68-71
Saints, representation of, 73-76, 83
Salviati, Francesco, 51, 69
Samacchini, Orazio, 51, 60, 64
San Lorenzo, Pontormo's frescoes for, 41
Santi di Tito, 51, 61, 62*n*, 66
Sarto, Andrea del: idealistic standardized attitude of, 5; influence on Pontormo, 20, 24; Dürer's influence on, 25-26; half figures in foreground, 27*n*; color treatment, 28; Florentine Mannerism developed from circle of, 41
Sculpture, Michelangelo's treatment of space in, 15

Sebastiano del Piombo, 19
Seven Works of Charity (Caravaggio), 67
Sistine Chapel, 14, 15-16
Sodoma, Il, 42n
Space: in *quattrocento* art, 4-5; problems in Mannerism, 8-9; Michelangelo's treatment of, 14-18; Rosso's treatment of, 32-33; Parmigianino's treatment of, 38-39, 40; in anti-Mannerism, 54-55
Stigmatization of St. Francis (Barocci), 74
Stigmatization of St. Francis (Cigoli), 74
Subjectivism, emphasis in Mannerism, 10, 10n
Supper at Emmaus (Caravaggio), 72-73
Supper at Emmaus (Moretto), 72
Supper at Emmaus (Pontormo), 72
Symmetry, breaking of, in Mannerism, 7

Themes, examination and characteristic development of, 68-76
Theory of art, 53
Times of Day (Michelangelo), 13
Titian: *Assumption of the Virgin,* 28;
influence on Lodovico Carracci, 59;
Supper at Emmaus, 72
Transfiguration (Rosso Fiorentino), 59
Transfiguration (Lodovico Carracci), 59-60
Transcendental element: in anti-Mannerism, 54, 55, 58, 77-78; in Annibale Carracci, 60-61; in Caravaggio, 67; in Rubens, 83
Trotti, Giovanni Battista, 67

Vasari, Giorgio: on German influence on Pontormo, 3-4, 25; *maniera* in, 48; as an artist "de petite manière," 51; *Immaculate Conception,* 56
Venetian School, 50-51, 71
Veronese, Paolo, 72
Verticalism: as characteristic of Mannerism, 10, 36; in Rosso Fiorentino, 30, 33; in Parmigianino, 36
Vertumnus and Pomona (Pontormo), 22-23
Victor (Michelangelo), 13, 42
Vision of St. Jerome (Parmigianino), 35, 37n
Visitation (Pontormo), 20
Volterra, Daniele da, 19

Zuccaro, Federigo, 10, 51, 53, 60
Zuccaro, Taddeo, 69